Korean Phrases with Cat Memes

First Edition: August 2017

ISBN: 978-1974216710

www.easy-korean.com

Contents

Preface

This book contains over 500 phrases in Korean. But, unlike other Korean phrase books, the expressions presented in this book are the same ones used by Korean speakers. That means you will be able to express yourself in 500 different ways without sounding unnatural. If everyone says, "Hey, how's it going?" you probably don't want to be saying, "Greetings, my good fellow. How are you doing these days?" Unfortunately, many phrases in other books are written this way. But this book is different.

Find Any Phrase in Seconds

The phrases in the first 18 chapters are written in English, which are then translated into Korean. This way you can find any phrase you are looking for in an instant. Each phrase has a box (□) that you can either check or circle, in case you want to find it later. The phrases are written in Hangul, the Korean alphabet, with the pronunciations provided in English.

Honorifics and Casual

Most phrases are written in two different styles; JDM and BM. JDM is short for 존댓말 (john-daet-mahl), also known as honorific speech. Basically, this is how people talk to strangers and the elderly in Korean. BM is 반말 (bahn-mahl), which is a casual style for talking to one's own siblings and close friends. (For more information on Korean grammar, please check out Korean Grammar with Cat Memes.)

Cat Memes! Because Why Not?

To make this book more fun, 35 "educational" cat memes are included. The memes were made with photos of two house cats, Soomba and Zorro. In case anyone is curious, here is a little bit of information on who they are.

Soomba (숨바꼭질)

Female

Loves tuna and chicken

Knows how to control her owner

Zorro (조로)

Male

Loves special treats

Toilet-trained, can open doors

1. Greetings & Introductions

☐ Hello / Hi

JDM: 안녕하세요. (Ahn-nyuhng-hah-seh-yoh.)

BM: 안녕. (Ahn-nyuhng.)

☐ It's nice to meet you / I'm glad to meet you

JDM: 반갑습니다. (Bahn-gahb-sseub-nee-dah.)

BM: 반갑다. (Bahn-gahb-ddah.)

☐ How are you? / How's it going?

JDM: 잘 계셨어요? (Jahl gyeah-shuh-ssuh-yoh?)

BM: 잘 있었어? (Jah ree-ssuh-ssuh?)

*Not for meeting someone for the first-time

☐ How have you been? / How are things?

JDM: 잘 지내시죠? (Jahl jee-nae-shee-jyoh?)

BM: 어떻게 지내? (Uh-dduh-keh jee-nae?)

*Not for meeting someone for the first-time

□ I'm glad to see you again / It's been a while

JDM: 오랜만입니다. (Oh-raen-mah-neeb-nee-dah.)

BM: 오랜만이다. (Oh-raen-mah-nee-dah.)

□ My name is <u>Mary</u> / I'm <u>Mary</u>

JDM: 전 <u>메리</u>예요. (Juhn <u>meh-ree</u>-yeah-yoh.)

BM: 난 <u>메리</u>야. (Nahn <u>meh-ree</u>-yah.)

☐ Are you <u>Choi Soo-cheol</u>? / You must be <u>Choi Soo-cheol</u>

JDM: <u>최수철</u> 님이세요? (<u>Chweh-soo-chuhl</u> nee-mee-seh-yoh?)

BM: 네가 <u>최수철</u>이니? (Neh-gah <u>chweh-soo-chuh</u>-ree-nee?)

☐ Welcome to <u>Korea</u>

JDM: <u>한국</u>에 잘 오셨어요. (<u>Hahn-goo</u>-geh jah roh-shuh-ssuh-yoh.)

BM: <u>한국</u> 잘 왔어. (<u>Hahn-goog</u> jjah rwah-ssuh.)

*For signs, 환영합니다 (hwah-nyuhng-hahb-nee-dah) should be written

☐ Let me introduce you to <u>Suzy</u>

JDM: <u>수지</u>를 소개해 드릴게요. (<u>Soo-jee</u>-reul soh-gae-hae deu-reel-ggeh-yoh.)

BM: <u>수지</u> 소개해줄게. (<u>Soo-jee</u> soh-gae-hae-jool-ggeh.)

*소개하다 (soh-gae-hah-dah) = introduce

☐ This is <u>Patrick</u> / I'd like you to meet <u>Patrick</u>

JDM: 이쪽은 <u>패트릭</u>이에요. (Ee-jjoh-geun <u>pae-teu-ree</u>-ghee-eh-yoh.)

BM: 여기는 <u>패트릭</u>이야. (Yuh-ghee-neun <u>pae-teu-ree</u>-ghee-yah.)

☐ I've heard a lot about you

JDM: 얘기 많이 들었습니다. (Yaeh-ghee mah-nee deu-ruht-sseub-nee-dah.)

BM: 얘기 많이 들었어. (Yaeh-ghee mah-nee deu-ruh-ssuh.)

□ I'm from <u>Italy</u> / I came from <u>Italy</u>

JDM: 전 <u>이탈리아</u>에서 왔어요. (Juh <u>nee-tahl-lee-ah</u>-eh-suh wah-ssuh-yoh.)

BM: 난 <u>이탈리아</u>에서 왔어. (Nah <u>nee-tahl-lee-ah</u>-eh-suh wah-ssuh.)

□ I'm glad you could come / I'm glad you came

JDM: 정말 잘 오셨어요. (Juhng-mahl jah roh-shuh-ssuh-yoh.)

BM: 정말 잘 왔어. (Juhng-mahl jah rwah-ssuh.)

*정말 (juhng-mahl) = really

□ I'm glad to be here

JDM: 와서 너무 좋아요. (Wah-suh nuh-moo joh-ah-yoh.)

BM: 와서 너무 좋아. (Wah-suh nuh-moo joh-ah.)

*너무 (nuh-moo) = very

□ What is your name?

JDM: 성함이 어떻게 되시죠? (Suhng-hah-mee uh-dduh-keh dweh-shee-jyoh?)

BM: 이름이 뭐야? (Ee-reu-mee mwuh-yah?)

□ I'll miss you / I'm going to miss you

JDM: 보고 싶을 거예요. (Boh-goh shee-peul gguh-yeah-yoh.)

BM: 보고 싶을 거야. (Boh-goh shee-peul gguh-yah.)

□ Bye

JDM: 안녕히 계세요. (Ahn-nyuhng-hee gyeah-seh-yoh.)

BM: 안녕. (Ahn-nyuhng.)

*When only the speaker is leaving

□ Bye / Get home safely

JDM: 들어가세요. (Deu-ruh-gah-seh-yoh.)

BM: 들어가. (Deu-ruh-gah.)

*When the listener or everyone is leaving

□ I'll see you later / See you next time

JDM: 다음에 봬요. (Dah-eu-meh bwae-yoh.)

BM: 다음에 봐. (Dah-eu-meh bwah.)

*다음 (dah-eum) = next time

□ Please take care / Take care

JDM: 건강하세요. (Guhn-gahng-hah-seh-yoh.)

BM: 건강해. (Guhn-gahng-hae.)

2. General Phrases

☐ Yes / Yes, I do / Yes, I am

JDM: 네. (Neh.)

BM: 어. (Uh.)

☐ No / No, I don't / No, I'm not

JDM: 아니요. (Ah-nee-yoh.)

BM: 아니. (Ah-nee.)

☐ Thank you / Thanks

JDM: 감사합니다. (Gahm-sah-hahb-nee-dah.)

BM: 고마워. (Goh-mah-wuh.)

☐ You're welcome / No problem / Don't mention it

JDM: 네. (Neh.)

BM: 어. (Uh.)

*Simply saying 'yes' or 'no' is a typical response to saying 'thank you'

□ I love you

JDM: 사랑해요. (Sah-rahng-hae-yoh.)

BM: 사랑해. (Sah-rahng-hae.)

□ Happy birthday

JDM: 생신 축하드려요. (Saeng-sheen choo-kah-deu-ryuh-yoh.)

BM: 생일 축하해. (Saeng-eel choo-kah-hae.)

□ Okay / All right

JDM: 네. (Neh.)

BM: 그래. (Geu-rae.)

□ Please

JDM: 제발이요. (Jeh-bah-ree-yoh.)

BM: 제발. (Jeh-bahl.)

*Not used often

□ Excuse me / Ma'am / Sir

JDM: 저기요. (Juh-ghee-yoh.)

□ Excuse me? / I'm sorry? / Can you repeat that?

JDM: 네? (Neh?)

BM: 어? (Uh?)

□ I'm sorry / Sorry

JDM: 죄송합니다. (Jweh-sohng-hahb-nee-dah.)

BM: 미안. (Mee-ahn.)

□ Sorry I'm late

JDM: 늦어서 죄송합니다. (Neu-juh-suh jweh-sohng-hahb-nee-dah.)

BM: 늦어서 미안. (Neu-juh-suh mee-ahn.)

□ That's okay / That's all right

JDM: 괜찮아요. (Gwaen-chah-nah-yoh.)

BM: 괜찮아. (Gwaen-chah-nah.)

□ Please wait / Just a moment

JDM: 잠깐만요. (Jahm-ggahn-mah-nyoh.)

BM: 잠깐만. (Jahm-ggahn-mahn.)

□ I don't know what you're saying / I can't understand you

JDM: 무슨 말씀인지 모르겠어요. (Moo-seun mahl-sseu-meen-jee moh-reu-geh-ssuh-yoh.)

BM: 무슨 말인지 모르겠어. (Moo-seun mah-reen-jee moh-reu-geh-ssuh.)

□ I don't speak Korean

JDM: 저 한국어 못해요. (Juh hahn-goo-guh moh-tae-yoh.)

BM: 나 한국어 못해. (Nah hahn-goo-guh moh-tae.)

*한국어 (hahn-goo-guh) = Korean language

□ My Korean is not very good / I only speak a little bit of Korean

JDM: 한국어 잘 몰아요. (Hahn-goo-guh jahl mohl-lah-yoh.)

BM: 한국어 잘 몰아. (Hahn-goo-guh jahl mohl-lah.)

□ I can speak Korean / I speak fluent Korean

JDM: 한국말 잘해요. (Hahn-goo-mahl jahl-hae-yoh.)

BM: 한국말 잘해. (Hahg-goo-mahl jahl-hae.)

*한국말 (hahn-goong-mahl) = Korean language

□ Your English is pretty good

JDM: 영어 잘하시네요. (Yuhng-uh jahl-hah-shee-neh-yoh.)

BM: 영어 잘하네. (Yuhng-uh jahl-hah-neh.)

□ I live in <u>New York</u> / My home is <u>New York</u>

JDM: 전 <u>뉴욕</u>에서 살아요. (Juhn <u>nyou-yoh</u>-geh-suh sah-rah-yoh.)

BM: <u>뉴욕</u> 살아. (<u>Nyou-yohg</u> ssah-rah.)

□ This is mine / It's mine

JDM: 제 거예요. (Jeh gguh-yeah-yoh.)

BM: 내 거야. (Nae gguh-yah.)

THIS IS MINE, JUST LIKE EVERYTHING ELSE YOU HAVE

□ I don't know / I'm not sure

JDM: 몰라요. (Mohl-lah-yoh.)

BM: 몰라. (Mohl-lah.)

□ I don't understand / I don't get it / I have no idea

JDM: 모르겠어요. (Moh-reu-geh-ssuh-yoh.)

BM: 모르겠어. (Moh-reu-geh-ssuh.)

□ I don't feel like it / Maybe not

JDM: 잘 모르겠어요. (Jahl moh-reu-geh-ssuh-yoh.)

BM: 잘 모르겠어. (Jahl moh-reu-geh-ssuh.)

□ I don't know, maybe

JDM: 글쎄요. (Geul-sseh-yoh.)

BM: 글쎄. (Geul-sseh.)

□ Good luck / Go get 'em

JDM: 화이팅. (Hwah-ee-ting.)

BM: 화이팅. (Hwah-ee-ting.)

□ Let's go

JDM: 가요. (Gah-yoh.)

BM: 가자. (Gah-jah.)

□ Wow / Oh my God

JDM: 와. (Wah.)

BM: 와. (Wah.)

□ That's great / That's fantastic

JDM: 잘됐네요. (Jahl-dwaet-neh-yoh.)

BM: 잘됐다. (Jahl-dwaet-ddah.)

□ Good job / Nice work

JDM: 잘하셨어요. (Jahl-hah-shuh-ssuh-yoh.)

BM: 잘했어. (Jahl-hae-ssuh.)

□ Great / I like it / I love it

JDM: 좋아요. (Joh-ah-yoh.)

BM: 좋아. (Joh-ah.)

□ I don't like it / I hate it

JDM: 싫어요. (Shee-ruh-yoh.)

BM: 싫어. (Shee-ruh.)

□ I don't mind / I don't really care

JDM: 괜찮아요. (Gwaen-chah-nah-yoh.)

BM: 상관없어. (Sahng-gwah-nuhb-ssuh.)

□ Oh no / That's terrible

JDM: 어떡해요. (Uh-dduh-kae-yoh.)

BM: 어떡헤. (Uh-dduh-kae.)

□ No way / That's unbelievable

JDM: 진짜요? (Jeen-jjah-yoh?)

BM: 말도 안 돼. (Mahl-doh ahn dwae.)

□ Right / That's right

JDM: 맞아요. (Mah-jah-yoh.)

BM: 맞아. (Mah-jah.)

□ Not really

JDM: 아뇨. (Ah-nyoh.)

BM: 아니. (Ah-nee.)

☐ Good morning

JDM: 일어나셨어요? (Ee-ruh-nah-shuh-ssuh-yoh?)

BM: 일어났어? (Ee-ruh-nah-ssuh?)

*일어나다 (ee-ruh-nah-dah) = wake up/get up

☐ Good night

JDM: 안녕히 주무세요. (Ahn-nyuhng-hee joo-moo-seh-yoh.)

BM: 잘 자. (Jahl jah.)

☐ I'll see you there / Let's meet there

JDM: 거기서 뵐게요. (Guh-ghee-suh bwehl-ggeh-yoh.)

BM: 거기서 만나. (Guh-ghee-suh mahn-dah.)

*거기 (guh-ghee) = there

☐ Congratulations

JDM: 축하합니다. (Choo-kah-hahb-nee-dah.)

BM: 축하해. (Choo-kah-hae.)

I BROKE THE VASE, CONGRATS!

NOW YOU DON'T HAVE TO WATER IT ANYMORE

☐ **Please hurry**

JDM: 서둘러 주세요. (Suh-dool-luh joo-seh-yoh.)

BM: 빨리빨리 해. (Bbahl-lee-bbahl-lee hae.)

☐ **Stop / Please stop doing that**

JDM: 하지 마세요. (Hah-jee mah-seh-yoh.)

BM: 하지 마. (Hah-jee mah.)

☐ **That's funny**

JDM: 웃겨요. (Woot-ggyuh-yoh.)

BM: 웃기다. (Woot-gghee-dah.)

□ That's interesting

JDM: 신기해요. (Sheen-ghee-hae-yoh.)

BM: 신기하다. (Sheen-ghee-hah-dah.)

□ This is fun

JDM: 재미있어요. (Jae-mee-ee-ssuh-yoh.)

BM: 재미있어. (Jae-mee-ee-ssuh.)

□ This is not fun

JDM: 재미없어요. (Jae-mee-uhb-ssuh-yoh.)

BM: 재미없어. (Jae-mee-uhb-ssuh.)

□ You're being too loud / That's too loud

JDM: 시끄러워요. (Shee-ggeu-ruh-wuh-yoh.)

BM: 시끄러워. (Shee-ggeu-ruh-wuh.)

□ Can you please tone it down? / Can you please be quiet?

JDM: 조용히 좀 해주세요. (Joh-yohng-hee johm hae-joo-seh-yoh.)

BM: 조용히 좀 해. (Joh-yohng-hee johm hae.)

☐ Do you have a religion?

JDM: 종교 있으세요? (Johng-gyoh ee-sseu-seh-yoh?)

BM: 종교 있니? (Johng-gyoh eet-nee?)

*종교 (johng-gyoh) = religion

☐ My religion is <u>Christianity</u>

JDM: 제 종교는 <u>기독교</u>예요. (Jeh johng-gyoh-neun <u>ghee-dohg-ggyoh</u>-yeah-yoh.)

BM: 내 종교는 <u>기독교</u>야. (Nae johng-gyoh-neun <u>ghee-dohg-ggyoh</u>-yah.)

☐ I don't have a religion / I'm an atheist

JDM: 저는 무종교예요. (Juh-neun moo-johng-gyoh-yeah-yoh.)

BM: 난 무종교야. (Nahn moo-johng-gyoh-yah.)

*무종교 (moo-johng-gyoh) = atheism/atheist

3. Common Questions

□ **Who?**

JDM: 누구요? (Noo-goo-yoh?)

BM: 누구? (Noo-goo?)

□ **What?**

JDM: 뭐라고요? (Mwuh-rah-goh-yoh?)

BM: 뭐? (Mwuh?)

□ **Where?**

JDM: 어디요? (Uh-dee-yoh?)

BM: 어디? (Uh-dee?)

□ **When?**

JDM: 언제요? (Uhn-jeh-yoh?)

BM: 언제? (Uhn-jeh?)

□ Why? / Why not? / How come?

JDM: 왜요? (Wae-yoh?)

BM: 왜? (Wae?)

□ How?

JDM: 어떻게요? (Uh-dduh-keh-yoh?)

BM: 어떻게? (Uh-dduh-keh?)

□ Which one?

JDM: 어떤 거요? (Uh-dduhn guh-yoh?)

BM: 어떤 거? (Uh-dduhn guh?)

□ So? / So what?

JDM: 그래서요? (Geu-rae-suh-yoh?)

BM: 그래서? (Geu-rae-suh?)

□ What is this?

JDM: 이게 뭐예요? (Ee-guh mwuh-yeah-yoh?)

BM: 이게 뭐야? (Ee-geh mwuh-yah?)

□ What is your phone number?

JDM: 전화번호가 뭐예요? (Juhn-hwah-buhn-hoh-gah mwuh-yeah-yoh?)

BM: 전화번호 뭐야? (Juhn-hwah-buhn-hoh mwuh-yah?)

*전화번호 (juhn-hwah-buhn-hoh) = phone number

□ Can I borrow your phone for a minute?

JDM: 잠시 전화 좀 빌릴 수 있을까요? (Jahm-shee juhn-hwah johm beel-leel ssoo ee-sseul-ggah-yoh?)

BM: 잠깐 전화 좀 빌려줄래? (Jahm-ggahn juhn-hwah johm beel-lyuh-jool-lae?)

*전화 (juhn-hwah) = phone

□ Where is it?

JDM: 어디 있어요? (Uh-dee ee-ssuh-yoh?)

BM: 어디 있어? (Uh-dee ee-ssuh?)

□ Who is it? / Who's there?

JDM: 누구세요? (Noo-goo-seh-yoh?)

□ How old are you?

JDM: 나이가 어떻게 되세요? (Nah-ee-gah uh-dduh-keh dweh-seh-yoh?)

BM: 몇 살이야? (Myuht ssah-ree-yah?)

□ How much is this? / How much?

JDM: 이거 얼마예요? (Ee-guh uhl-mah-yeah-yoh?)

BM: 이거 얼마야? (Ee-guh uhl-mah-yah?)

*이거 (ee-guh) = this

□ How about you? / What about you?

JDM: 어떠세요? (Uh-dduh-seh-yoh?)

BM: 너는 어때? (Nuh-neun uh-ddae?)

□ Are you sure?

JDM: 확실한 건가요? (Hwahg-sseel-hahn guhn-gah-yoh?)

BM: 확실해? (Hwahg-sseel-hae?)

□ Are you married?

JDM: 결혼하셨어요? (Gyuhl-hohn-hah-shuh-ssuh-yoh?)

BM: 결혼했어? (Gyuhl-hohn-hae-ssuh?)

*결혼하다 (gyuhl-hohn-hah-dah) = get married

□ Do you have children?

JDM: 아이가 있으신가요? (Ah-ee-gah ee-sseu-sheen-gah-yoh?)

BM: 아이 있어? (Ah-ee ee-ssuh?)

□ Do you speak <u>English</u>?

JDM: <u>영어</u> 하세요? (<u>Yuhng-uh</u> hah-seh-yoh?)

BM: <u>영어</u> 하니? (<u>Yuhng-uh</u> hah-nee?)

□ Do you know someone who speaks English?

JDM: 영어 하는 사람 아세요? (Yuhng-uh hah-neun sah-rah mah-seh-yoh?)

BM: 영어 하는 사람 알아? (Yuhng-uh hah-neun sah-rah mah-rah?)

☐ What does this mean in English?

JDM: 영어로는 뜻이 뭐예요? (Yuhng-uh-roh-neun ddeu-shee mwuh-yeah-yoh?)

BM: 영어로는 뜻이 뭐야? (Yuhng-uh-roh-neun ddeu-shee mwuh-yah?)

*뜻 (ddeut) = meaning

☐ Have you been to <u>Malaysia</u>?

JDM: <u>말레이시아</u>에 가보신 적 있으세요? (<u>Mahl-leh-ee-shee-ah</u>-eh gah-boh-sheen guh ghee-sseu-heh-yoh?)

BM: <u>말레이시아</u>에 가본 적 있어? (<u>Mahl-leh-ee-shee-ah</u>-eh gah-bohn juh ghee-ssuh?)

☐ Is This <u>Seoul</u>? / Am I in <u>Seoul</u>?

JDM: 여기가 <u>서울</u>인가요? (Yuh-ghee-gah <u>suh-woo</u>-reen-gah-yoh?)

BM: 여기가 <u>서울</u>이야? (Yuh-ghee-gah <u>suh-woo</u>-ree-yah?)

*여기 (yuh-ghee) = here

☐ What do you do for a living?

JDM: 직업이 어떻게 되세요? (Jee-guh-bee uh-dduh-keh dweh-seh-yoh?)

BM: 무슨 일 해? (Moo-seu neel hae?)

☐ What school do you go to?

JDM: 학교 어디 다니세요? (Hahg-ggyoh uh-dee dah-nee-seh-yoh?)

BM: 학교 어디 다녀? (Hahg-ggyoh uh-dee dah-nyuh?)

*학교 (hahg-ggyoh) = school

☐ What is your favorite <u>food</u>? / What kind of <u>food</u> do you like?

JDM: 어떤 <u>음식</u> 좋아하세요? (Uh-dduh neum-sheeg joh-ah-hah-seh-yoh?)

BM: <u>음식</u> 뭐 좋아해? (Eum-sheeg mwuh joh-ah-hae?)

☐ Do you like <u>dogs</u>?

JDM: <u>개</u> 좋아하세요? (<u>Gae</u> joh-ah-hah-seh-yoh?)

BM: <u>개</u> 좋아해? (<u>Gae</u> joh-ah-hae?)

*좋아하다 (joh-ah-hah-dah) = like/love

□ Do you know <u>Adele</u>?

JDM: 혹시 <u>아델</u> 아세요? (Hohg-ssee <u>ah-deh</u> rah-seh-yoh?)

BM: 혹시 <u>아델</u> 알아? (Hohg-ssee <u>ah-deh</u> rah-rah?)

*혹시 (hohg-ssee) = perhaps

□ Would you like some <u>coffee</u>?

JDM: <u>커피</u> 좀 드릴까요? (<u>Kuh-pee</u> johm deu-reel-ggah-yoh?)

BM: <u>커피</u> 줄까? (<u>Kuh-pee</u> jool-ggah?)

□ Which one is better? / Which one do you like more?

JDM: 어떤 게 더 나아요? (Uh-dduhn geh duh nah-ah-yoh?)

BM: 어떤 게 더 나아? (Uh-dduhn geh duh nah-ah?)

□ What do you think? / What is your opinion?

JDM: 어떻게 생각하세요? (Uh-dduh-keh saeng-gah-kah-seh-yoh?)

BM: 어떻게 생각해? (Uh-dduh-keh saeng-gah-kae?)

*생각하다 (saeng-gah-kah-dah) = think

□ What are your hobbies?

JDM: 취미가 어떻게 되세요? (Chwee-mee-gah uh-dduh-keh dweh-seh-yoh?)

BM: 넌 취미가 뭐야? (Nuhn chwee-mee-gah mwuh-yah?)

*취미 (chwee-mee) = hobby

□ Really? / Are you serious?

JDM: 진짜요? (Jeen-jjah-yoh?)

BM: 진짜? (Jeen-jjah?)

□ May I? / Is that all right?

JDM: 괜찮아요? (Gwaen-chah-nah-yoh?)

BM: 그래도 돼? (Geu-rae-doh dwae?)

□ Can you take a photo of me?

JDM: 사진 좀 찍어 주시겠어요? (Sah-jeen johm jjee-guh joo-shee-geh-ssuh-yoh?)

BM: 사진 좀 찍어 줄래? (Sah-jeen johm jjee-guh jool-lae?)

*사진 (sah-jeen) = photograph

□ Are you okay? / Are you all right?

JDM: 괜찮으세요? (Gwaen-chah-neu-seh-yoh?)

BM: 괜찮아? (Gwaen-chah-nah?)

□ Can you please help me?

JDM: 저 좀 도와주시겠어요? (Juh johm doh-wah-joo-shee-geh-ssuh-yoh?)

BM: 나 좀 도와줄래? (Nah johm doh-wah-jool-lae?)

*도와주다 (doh-wah-joo-dah) = help

□ What's the problem? / What seems to be the problem?

JDM: 무슨 문제예요? (Moo-seun moon-jeh-yeah-yoh?)

BM: 무슨 문제야? (Moo-seun moon-jeh-yah?)

*문제 (moon-jeh) = problem/issue

☐ Is that not allowed? / Is that a problem?

JDM: 그러면 안 돼나요? (Geu-ruh-myuh nahn dwae-nah-yoh?)

BM: 그러면 안 돼? (Geu-ruh-myuh nahn dwae?)

☐ Is it okay to <u>smoke</u>?

JDM: <u>담배 피워도</u> 돼요? (<u>Dahm-bae pee-wuh</u>-doh dwae-yoh?)

BM: <u>담배 피워도</u> 돼? (<u>Dahm-bae pee-wuh</u>-doh dwae?)

*담배 (dahm-bae) = cigarette

☐ Does this have <u>meat</u> in it? / Is there <u>meat</u> in it?

JDM: 여기 <u>고기</u> 들어갔어요? (Yuh-ghee <u>goh-ghee</u> deu-ruh-gah-ssuh-yoh?)

BM: 여기 <u>고기</u> 들어갔어? (Yuh-ghee <u>goh-ghee</u> deu-ruh-gah-ssuh?)

4. Air & Travel

☐ What is the purpose of your visit?

JDM: 방문하신 목적이 무엇인가요? (Bahng-moon-hah-sheen mohg-jjuh-ghee moo-uh-sheen-gah-yoh?)

*목적 (mohg-jjuhg) = purpose/reason

☐ I'm here for <u>vacation</u>

JDM: <u>여행</u>하러 왔어요. (<u>Yuh-haeng</u>-hah-ruh wah-ssuh-yoh.)

☐ I'm staying for <u>3 weeks</u>

JDM: <u>3주</u> 동안 머물 거예요. (<u>Sahm-joo</u> dohng-ahn muh-mool gguh-yeah-yoh.)

☐ I want to check my luggage / You can check the luggage

JDM: 짐은 부쳐 주세요. (Jee-meun boo-chuh joo-seh-yoh.)

*짐 (jeem) = luggage/baggage

☐ I'm not checking my luggage / I'll carry the luggage

JDM: 짐은 안 부쳐요. (Jee-meu nahn boo-chuh-yoh.)

□ When do we board the plane?

JDM: 탑승은 언제 하나요? (Tahb-sseung-eu nuhn-jeh hah-nah-yoh?)

*탑승 (tahb-sseung) = boarding

□ I'm looking for my gate

JDM: 게이트를 찾고 있어요. (Geh-ee-teu-reul chaht-ggoh ee-ssuh-yoh.)

□ I'm transferring to another flight

JDM: 다른 비행기로 갈아탈 거예요. (Dah-reun bee-haeng-ghee-roh gah-rah-tahl gguh-yeah-yoh.)

*갈아타다 (gah-rah-tah-dah) = transfer

□ My luggage is missing

JDM: 제 짐이 분실됐어요. (Jeh jee-mee boon-sheel-dwae-ssuh-yoh.)

*짐 (jeem) = luggage

□ I can't find my boarding pass

JDM: 제 탑승권을 못 찾겠어요. (Jeh tahb-sseung-ggwuh-ncul moht chaht-ggeh-ssuh-yoh.)

*탑승권 (tahb-sseung-ggwuhn) = boarding pass

☐ I can't find the baggage claim area

JDM: 수하물 찾는 곳을 못 찾겠어요. (Soo-hah-mool chaht-neun goh-seul moht chaht-ggeh-ssuh-yoh.)

☐ I think I've lost my passport

JDM: 여권을 잃어버린 거 같아요. (Yuh-gguh-neu ree-ruh-buh-reen guh gah-tah-yoh.)

*여권 (yuh-gguhn) = passport

☐ I think I missed my flight

JDM: 비행기를 놓친 거 같아요. (Bee-haeng-ghee-reul noh-cheen guh gah-tah-yoh.)

☐ I think I'm lost

JDM: 길을 잃은 거 같아요. (Ghee-reu ree-reun guh gah-tah-yoh.)

☐ I'm looking for the restroom / Do you know where the bathroom is?

JDM: 화장실을 찾고 있어요. (Hwah-jahng-shee-reul chaht-ggoh ee-ssuh-yoh.)

*화장실 (hwah-jahng-sheel) = bathroom/restroom

☐ How do I get to the exit?

JDM: 출구로 가려면 어떻게 해요? (Chool-goo-roh gah-ryuh-myuh nuh-dduh-keh hae-yoh?)

*출구 (chool-goo) = exit

□ My Korean is not very good

JDM: 한국말을 잘 못해요. (Hahn-goong-mah-reul jahl moh-tae-yoh.)

*한국말 (hahn-goong-mahl) = Korean language

□ What does this mean in English?

JDM: 영어로는 무슨 뜻이에요? (Yuhng-uh-roh-neun moo-seun ddeu-shee-eh-yoh?)

*영어 (yuhng-uh) = English

□ I don't have any Korean money

JDM: 한국 돈이 없어요. (Hahn-goog ddoh-nee uhb-ssuh-yoh.)

*돈 (dohn) = money

□ I have <u>500 dollars</u>

JDM: <u>500달러</u> 있어요. (<u>Oh-baeg-ddahl-luh</u> ee-ssuh-yoh.)

□ Do you accept credit cards?

JDM: 신용카드로 계산 되나요? (Shee-nyohng-kah-deu-roh gyeah-sahn dweh-nah-yoh?)

*신용카드 (shee-nyohng-kah-deu) = credit card

☐ Keep the change

JDM: 거스름돈은 됐어요. (Guh-seu-reum-ddoh-neun dwae-ssuh-yoh.)

*거스름돈 (guh-seu-reum-ddohn) = change

☐ Can I get a refund?

JDM: 환불 가능한가요? (Hwahn-bool gah-neung-hahn-gah-yoh?)

*환불 (hwahn-bool) = refund

☐ Where is the <u>bus station</u>?

JDM: 버스 정류장이 어디에요? (<u>Buh-sseu juhng-nyou-jahng</u>-ee uh-dee-eh-yoh?)

☐ How do I get to <u>Busan</u>? / How can I go to <u>Busan</u>?

JDM: 부산으로 어떻게 가요? (<u>Boo-sah</u>-neu-roh uh-dduh-keh gah-yoh?)

☐ How long does it take?

JDM: 얼마나 걸려요? (Uhl-mah-nah guhl-lyuh-yoh?)

☐ How do I get to a <u>hotel</u>?

JDM: 호텔에는 어떻게 가죠? (<u>Hoh-teh</u>-reh-neu nuh-dduh-keh gah-jyoh?)

☐ Does this <u>train</u> go to Seoul?

JDM: 이 <u>기차</u> 서울로 가요? (Ee <u>ghee-chah</u> suh-wool-loh gah-yoh?)

☐ When is the <u>train</u> coming?

JDM: <u>기차</u> 언제 와요? (<u>Ghee-chah</u> uhn-jeh wah-yoh?)

☐ Do you have any available seats?

JDM: 빈 좌석이 있나요? (Been jwah-suh-ghee eet-nah-yoh?)

☐ Can I get another seat?

JDM: 다른 자리로 바꿀 수 있나요? (Dah-reun jah-ree-roh bah-ggool ssoo eet-nah-yoh?)

*자리 (jah-ree) = seat

☐ Is this seat taken?

JDM: 이 자리 누구 있나요? (Ee jah-ree noo-goo eet-nah-yoh?)

☐ Is there a <u>subway station</u> around here?

JDM: 주변에 <u>지하철역</u>이 있나요? (Joo-byuh-neh <u>jee-hah-chuhl-lyuh</u>-ghee eet-nah-yoh?)

*주변 (joo-byuhn) = vicinity

☐ Do you have a subway map?

JDM: 지하철 노선도 있으세요? (Jee-hah-chuhl noh-suhn-doh ee-sseu-seh-yoh?)

☐ How do I transfer to <u>Line 2</u>?

JDM: <u>2호선</u>으로 어떻게 갈아타죠? (<u>Ee-hoh-suh</u>-neu-roh uh-dduh-keh gah-rah-tah-jyoh?)

☐ Excuse me, is the next stop <u>Jongno Station</u>?

JDM: 저기, 다음 역이 <u>종로역</u> 맞나요? (Juh-ghee, dah-eu myuh-ghee <u>johng-noh-yuhg</u> maht-nah-yoh?)

☐ Does this bus go to <u>Yongsan</u>?

JDM: 이 버스 <u>용산</u> 가요? (Ee buh-sseu <u>yohng-sahn</u> gah-yoh?)

☐ Which bus should I take for <u>Itaewon</u>?

JDM: <u>이태원</u> 가려면 몇 번 타요? (<u>Ee-tae-wuhn</u> gah-ryuh-myuhn myuht bbuhn tah-yoh?)

*몇 번 (myuht bbuhn) = what number/which bus

☐ <u>Seoul Station</u>, please / Please take me to <u>Seoul Station</u>

JDM: <u>서울역</u>이요. (<u>Suh-wool-lyuh</u>-ghee-yoh.)

*역 (yuhg) = station

□ **I need to get to this address / This is where I need to go**

JDM: 이 곳으로 가주세요. (Ee goh-seu-roh gah-joo-seh-yoh.)

□ **How much do I owe you? / How much is the fare?**

JDM: 요금이 얼마예요? (Yoh-geu-mee uhl-mah-yeah-yoh?)

*요금 (yoh-geum) = fare/fee

□ **Should I give you a tip? / Do I need to tip?**

JDM: 팁 드려야 하나요? (Teeb ddeu-ryuh-yah hah-nah-yoh?)

*Tipping is not expected in Korea

□ **Can you please slow down? / You're going too fast**

JDM: 천천히 가주세요. (Chuhn-chuhn-hee gah-joo-seh-yoh.)

*천천히 (chuhn-chuhn-hee) = slowly/not too fast

□ **Can you pull over there, please? / I'll get out here**

JDM: 저기에 세워주세요. (Juh-ghee-eh seh-wuh-joo-seh-yoh.)

□ **This is my stop**

JDM: 저 여기에서 내려요. (Juh yuh-ghee-eh-suh nae-ryuh-yoh.)

*여기 (yuh-ghee) = here

5. Directions

□ **Do you know how to get to <u>Dongdaemun</u>?**

JDM: <u>동대문</u>에 어떻게 가요? (<u>Dohng-dae-moo</u>-neh uh-dduh-keh gah-yoh?)

□ **How do I go to <u>Hongdae</u> from here?**

JDM: <u>홍대</u>에 가려면 어떻게 해요? (<u>Hohng-dae</u>-eh gah-ryuh-myuh nuh-dduh-keh hae-yoh?)

□ **Can you show me where <u>Itaewon</u> is? / Where is <u>Itaewon</u> on this map?**

JDM: <u>이태원</u>이 여기 어디에요? (<u>Ee-tae-wuh</u>-nee yuh-ghee uh-dee-eh-yoh?)

*여기 (yuh-ghee) = here

□ **I'm trying to find this place / How can I go here?**

JDM: 여기를 찾고 있어요. (Yuh-ghee-reul chaht-ggoh ee-ssuh-yoh.)

□ **Is <u>Insadong</u> this way?**

JDM: <u>인사동</u>이 이쪽인가요? (<u>Een-sah-dohng</u>-ee ee-jjoh-gheen-gah-yoh?)

□ I can't seem to find <u>Myeongdong</u> / I'm looking for <u>Myeongdong</u>

JDM: <u>명동</u>을 못 찾겠어요. (<u>Myuhng-dohng</u>-eul moht chaht-ggeh-ssuh-yoh.)

□ How far away is it from here?

JDM: 여기서 얼마나 멀어요? (Yuh-ghee-suh uhl-mah-nah muh-ruh-yoh?)

□ It's not that far

JDM: 별로 안 멀어요. (Byuhl-loh ahn muh-ruh-yoh.)

*별로 (byuhl-loh) = not much

□ It's a little too far from here

JDM: 여기서는 너무 멀어요. (Yuh-ghee-suh-neun nuh-moo muh-ruh-yoh.)

□ Follow me

JDM: 따라오세요. (Ddah-rah-oh-seh-yoh.)

□ It's about <u>10 minutes</u> from here

JDM: 여기서 한 <u>10분</u>쯤 걸려요. (Yuh-ghee-suh hahn <u>sheeb-bboon</u>-jjeum guhl-lyuh-yoh.)

□ It's <u>three blocks</u> away

JDM: <u>세 블록</u> 가시면 돼요. (<u>Seh beul-lohg</u> gah-shee-myuhn dwae-yoh.)

□ I don't know where that is

JDM: 잘 모르겠는데요. (Jahl moh-reu-geht-neun-deh-yoh.)

*잘 (jahl) = well

□ Is this way east or west?

JDM: 이쪽이 동쪽인가요 서쪽인가요? (Ee-jjoh-ghee dohng-jjoh-gheen-gah-yoh suh-jjoh-gheen-gah-yoh?)

□ Is this way north or south?

JDM: 이쪽이 북쪽인가요 남쪽인가요? (Ee-jjoh-ghee boog-jjoh-gheen-gah-yoh nahm-jjoh-gheen-gah-yoh?)

□ Go straight

JDM: 앞으로 쭉 가세요. (Ah-peu-roh jjoog ggah-seh-yoh.)

YES, GO STRAIGHT

UNTIL YOU FALL OFF A CLIFF!

☐ Turn left

JDM: 왼쪽으로 가세요. (Wehn-jjoh-geu-roh gah-seh-yoh.)

☐ Turn right

JDM: 오른쪽으로 가세요. (Oh-reun-jjoh-geu-roh gah-seh-yoh.)

☐ It's near the <u>post office</u>

JDM: <u>우체국</u> 근처에 있어요. (<u>Woo-cheh-goog</u> geun-chuh-eh ee-ssuh-yoh.)

☐ Go past the <u>bus station</u>

JDM: <u>버스 정류장</u>을 지나가세요. (<u>Buh-sseu juhng-nyou-jahng</u>-eul jee-nah-gah-seh-yoh.)

6. Numbers

☐ **Just <u>one</u>, please / I only need <u>one</u>**

JDM: 하나만 주세요. (<u>Hah-nah</u>-mahn joo-seh-yoh.)

☐ **This is the <u>second</u> time / This is my <u>second</u> visit**

JDM: 이번이 두 번째예요. (Ee-buh-nee <u>doo</u> buhn-jjae-yeah-yoh.)

BM: 이번이 두 번째야. (Ee-buh-nee <u>doo</u> buhn-jjae-yah.)

☐ **I'd like to buy <u>three</u> / Give me <u>three</u>**

JDM: 세 개 주세요. (<u>Seh</u> gae joo-seh-yoh.)

*개 (gae) = unit for counting things

☐ **I have <u>four</u> brothers and sisters / I have <u>four</u> siblings**

JDM: 형제자매가 네 명이에요. (Hyuhng-jeh-jah-mae-gah <u>neh</u> myuhng-ee-eh-yoh.)

BM: 형제자매가 네 명이야. (Hyuhng-jeh-jah-mae-gah <u>neh</u> myuhng-ee-yah.)

*명 (myuhng) = unit for counting people

□ I need <u>five</u> more / I'd like <u>five</u> more

JDM: <u>다섯</u> 개 더요. (<u>Dah-suht</u> ggae duh-yoh.)

BM: <u>다섯</u> 개 더. (<u>Dah-suht</u> ggae duh.)

*더 (duh) = more

□ Did you say '<u>six</u>?'

JDM: '<u>육</u>'이요? ('<u>You</u>'-ghee-yoh?)

BM: '<u>육</u>?' ('<u>Youg</u>?')

□ She is <u>seven</u> years old

JDM: 그녀는 <u>일곱</u> 살이에요. (Geu-nyuh-neu <u>neel-gohg</u> ssah-ree-eh-yoh.)

BM: 그녀는 <u>일곱</u> 살이야. (Geu-nyuh-neu <u>neel-gohg</u> ssah-ree-yah.)

*살 (sahl) = years old

□ They have <u>eight</u> members

JDM: 멤버는 <u>여덟</u> 명이에요. (Mehm-buh-neu <u>nyuh-duhl</u> myuhng-ee-eh-yoh.)

BM: 멤버는 <u>여덟</u> 명이야. (Mehm-buh-neu <u>nyuh-duhl</u> myuhng-ee-yah.)

THEY HAVE EIGHT MEMBERS

HOW COME I'M NOT ONE OF THEM?

□ My phone number is '02-345-6789'

JDM: 제 번호는 '02-345-6789'입니다. (Jeh buhn-hoh-neun 'gohng-ee-sahm-sah-oh-ryoug-cheel-pahl-goo'-eeb-nee-dah.)

BM: 내 번호는 '02-345-6789'야. (Nae buhn-hoh-neun 'gohng-ee-sahm-sah-oh-ryoug-cheel-pahl-goo'-yah.)

*번호 (buhn-hoh) = number/phone number

□ I have ten more

JDM: 열 개 더 있어요. (Yuhl ggae duh ee-ssuh-yoh.)

BM: 열 개 더 있어. (Yuhl ggae duh ee-ssuh.)

☐ It's less than a __hundred__

JDM: 백보다는 적어요. (<u>Baeg</u>-bboh-dah-neun juh-guh-yoh.)

BM: 백보다는 적어. (<u>Baeg</u>-bboh-dah-neun juh-guh.)

☐ I only have a __thousand__ won

JDM: 천 원밖에 없어요. (<u>Chuh</u> nwuhn-bah-ggeh uhb-ssuh-yoh.)

BM: 천 원밖에 없어. (<u>Chuh</u> nwuhn-bah-ggeh uhb-ssuh.)

*1,000 won = approx. $1 USD

☐ It's __ten-thousand__ won / It costs __ten-thousand__ won

JDM: 만 원입니다. (<u>Mah</u> nwuh-neeb-nee-dah.)

BM: 만 원. (<u>Mah</u> nwuhn.)

*만 (mahn) = 10,000

7. Money & Banks

☐ Is there a currency exchange booth nearby?

JDM: 여기 근처에 환전소 있나요? (Yuh-ghee geun-chuh-eh hwahn-juhn-soh eet-nah-yoh?)

*환전소 (hwahn-juhn-soh) = currency exchange booth

☐ I'd like to exchange <u>200 dollars</u>

JDM: <u>200달러</u> 환전이요. (<u>Ee-baeg-ddahl-luh</u> hwahn-juh-nee-yoh.)

*환전 (hwahn-juhn) = currency exchange

☐ What is the currency rate?

JDM: 환율이 어떻게 되나요? (Hwah-nyou-ree uh-dduh-keh dweh-nah-yoh?)

☐ I don't have any Korean money with me right now

JDM: 지금 한국 돈이 하나도 없어요. (Jee-geum hahn-goog ddoh-nee hah-nah-doh uhb-ssuh-yoh.)

BM: 지금 한국 돈이 하나도 없어. (Jee-geum hahn-goog ddoh-nee hah-nah-doh uhb-ssuh.)

*지금 (jee-geum) = right now

□ I don't have a lot of money / I'm running short of money

JDM: 돈이 별로 없어요. (Doh-nee byuhl-loh uhb-ssuh-yoh.)

BM: 돈이 별로 없어. (Doh-nee byuhl-loh uhb-ssuh.)

*돈 (dohn) = money

□ I have enough money

JDM: 돈이 충분히 있어요. (Doh-nee choong-boo-nee ee-ssuh-yoh.)

BM: 돈 충분히 있어. (Dohn choong-boo-nee ee-ssuh.)

□ I don't have any cash

JDM: 현금이 하나도 없어요. (Hyuhn-geu-mee hah-nah-doh uhb-ssuh-yoh.)

BM: 현금이 하나도 없어. (Hyuhn-geu-mee hah-nah-doh uhb-ssuh.)

*현금 (hyuhn-geum) = cash

□ How much?

JDM: 얼마예요? (Uhl-mah-yeah-yoh?)

BM: 얼마야? (Uhl-mah-yah?)

□ Can I pay with a credit card?

JDM: 카드로 계산되나요? (Kah-deu-roh gyeah-sahn-dweh-nah-yoh?)

□ I'd like to open a bank account

JDM: 계좌를 새로 만들고 싶어요. (Gyeah-jwah-reul sae-roh mahn-deul-goh shee-puh-yoh.)

*계좌 (gyeah-jwah) = bank account

□ Can I get a debit card?

JDM: 체크카드를 만들 수 있나요? (Cheh-keu-kah-deu-reul mahn-deul ssoo eet-nah-yoh?)

*체크카드 (cheh-keu-kah-deu) = debit card

□ Is there a fee?

JDM: 수수료가 있나요? (Soo-soo-ryoh-gah eet-nah-yoh?)

*수수료 (soo-soo-ryoh) = fee/charge

□ I'd like online banking services

JDM: 인터넷 뱅킹을 사용하고 싶어요. (Een-tuh-neht baeng-king-eul sah-yohng-hah-goh shee-puh-yoh.)

□ I'd like to make a deposit

JDM: 입금해 주세요. (Eeb-ggeum-hae joo-seh-yoh.)

*입금 (eeb-ggeum) = deposit

□ I'd like to withdraw <u>2,000 dollars</u>

JDM: <u>2,000불</u> 인출해 주세요. (<u>Ee-chuhn-boo</u> reen-chool-hae joo-seh-yoh.)

*불 (bool) = dollar

□ I'd like to wire some money

JDM: 돈 송금하려고요. (Dohn sohng-geum-hah-ryuh-goh-yoh.)

*송금 (sohng-geum) = wire transfer

□ Is there an ATM machine?

JDM: 여기 ATM 기기가 있나요? (Yuh-ghee eh-ee-tee-ehm ghee-ghee-gah eet-nah-yoh?)

□ When does the bank open? / What time does the bank open?

JDM: 은행이 몇시에 문 여나요? (Eun-haeng-ee myuht-ssee-eh moo nyuh-nah-yoh?)

*은행 (eun-haeng) = bank

□ When does the bank close? / What time does the bank close?

JDM: 은행이 몇시에 문 닫나요? (Eun-haeng-ee myuht-ssee-eh moon daht-nah-yoh?)

8. Shopping

☐ Let's go shopping / I want to go shopping

JDM: 쇼핑하러 가요. (Ssyoh-ping-hah-ruh gah-yoh.)

BM: 쇼핑 가자. (Ssyoh-ping gah-jah.)

☐ Do you want to go shopping tomorrow?

JDM: 내일 쇼핑하러 가실래요? (Nae-eel ssyoh-ping-hah-ruh gah-sheel-lae-yoh?)

BM: 내일 쇼핑하러 갈래? (Nae-eel ssyoh-ping-hah-ruh gahl-lae?)

*내일 (nae-eel) = tomorrow

☐ I need to buy some <u>clothes</u>

JDM: <u>옷</u>을 좀 사야 돼요. (<u>Oh</u>-seul johm sah-yah dwae-yoh.)

BM: <u>옷</u> 좀 사야 돼. (<u>Oht</u> jjohm sah-yah dwae.)

☐ Where can I buy some <u>shoes</u>?

JDM: <u>신발</u>은 어디에서 사요? (<u>Sheen-bah</u>-reu nuh-dee-eh-suh sah-yoh?)

BM: <u>신발</u>은 어디에서 사? (<u>Sheen-bah</u>-reu nuh-dee-eh-suh sah?)

☐ It doesn't fit

JDM: 안 맞아요. (Ahn mah-jah-yoh.)

☐ It's too big

JDM: 너무 커요. (Nuh-moo kuh-yoh.)

*너무 (nuh-moo) = too/very

☐ It's too small

JDM: 너무 작아요. (Nuh-moo jah-gah-yoh.)

□ It's too loose

JDM: 너무 헐거워요. (Nuh-moo huhl-guh-wuh-yoh.)

□ It's too tight

JDM: 너무 꽉 껴요. (Nuh-moo ggwahg ggyuh-yoh.)

□ Do you have one size smaller?

JDM: 한 사이즈 작은 거 있어요? (Hahn ssah-ee-jeu jah-geun guh ee-ssuh-yoh?)

□ Do you have one size bigger?

JDM: 한 사이즈 큰 거 있어요? (Hahn ssah-ee-jeu keun guh ee-ssuh-yoh?)

□ Does this come in another color? / Is there a different color?

JDM: 다른 색도 있어요? (Dah-reun saeg-ddoh ee-ssuh-yoh?)

*색 (saeg) = color

□ I'm just browsing / I'm just looking

JDM: 그냥 구경해요. (Geu-nyahng goo-gyuhng-hae-yoh.)

☐ How much is it? / What's the price?

JDM: 얼마예요? (Uhl-mah-yeah-yoh?)

BM: 얼마야? (Uhl-mah-yah?)

☐ How much is the total? / What's the total?

JDM: 다 해서 얼마예요? (Dah hae-suh uhl-mah-yeah-yoh?)

☐ It's a little too expensive / It's too pricey

JDM: 너무 비싸요. (Nuh-moo bee-ssah-yoh.)

*비싸다 (bee-ssah-dah) = expensive

☐ Can you lower the price, please?

JDM: 깎아 주세요. (Ggah-ggah joo-seh-yoh.)

☐ Can I get a receipt? / I'd like a receipt

JDM: 영수증 있나요? (Yuhng-soo-jeung eet-nah-yoh?)

*영수증 (yuhng-soo-jeung) = receipt

□ When does your shop close? / What time do you close?

JDM: 몇 시에 문 닫으세요? (Myuht ssee-eh moon dah-deu-seh-yoh?)

□ Is this refundable? / Can I get a refund later?

JDM: 나중에 환불 가능한가요? (Nah-joong-eh hwahn-bool gah-neung-hahn-gah-yoh?)

*환불 (hwahn-bool) = refund

□ I'd like to get a refund / I want a refund

JDM: 환불해 주세요. (Hwahn-bool-hae joo-seh-yoh.)

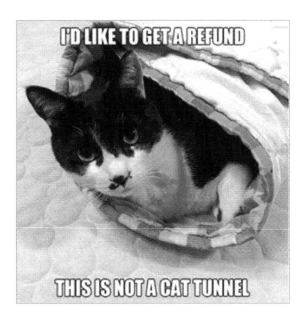

☐ This product has a flaw / There's something is wrong with this

JDM: 제품에 하자가 있어요. (Jeh-poo-meh hah-jah-gah ee-ssuh-yoh.)

*하자 (hah-jah) = flaw/defect

☐ I want to exchange this with something else

JDM: 다른 걸로 바꿔 주세요. (Dah-reun guhl-loh bah-ggwuh joo-seh-yoh.)

☐ I'll come back later

JDM: 둘러보고 올게요. (Dool-luh-boh-goh ohl-ggeh-yoh.)

9. Food & Restaurants

☐ A table for two, please

JDM: 두 명이요. (Doo myuhng-ee-yoh.)

☐ I have a reservation

JDM: 예약했어요. (Yeah-yah-kae-ssuh-yoh.)

*예약하다 (yeah-yah-kah-dah) = make a reservation

☐ Do you have a menu? / Can I get a menu?

JDM: 메뉴판 있으세요? (Meh-nyou-pah nee-sseu-seh-yoh?)

☐ We'd like a minute before we order

JDM: 조금 있다가 주문할게요. (Joh-geu meet-ddah-gah joo-moon-hahl-ggeh-yoh.)

*주문하다 (joo-moon-hah-dah) = order

☐ What is good here? / What do you recommend?

JDM: 뭐가 맛있어요? (Mwuh-gah mah-shee-ssuh-yoh?)

☐ Do you have any specials?

JDM: 스페셜 있어요? (Seu-peh-shuh ree-ssuh-yoh?)

☐ What is in this meal? / What are the ingredients?

JDM: 안에 뭐가 들어갔어요? (Ah-neh mwuh-gah deu-ruh-gah-ssuh-yoh?)

☐ What is this called? / What is the name of this?

JDM: 이건 뭐라고 해요? (Ee-guhn mwuh-rah-goh hae-yoh?)

*이거 (ee-guh) = this

☐ I'm allergic to shrimp / I can't eat shrimp

JDM: 새우 알러지 때문에 못 먹어요. (Sae-woo ahl-luh-jee ddae-moo-neh moht muh-guh-yoh.)

□ **I'm a vegetarian / I'm a vegan / I don't eat meat**

JDM: 저는 채식주의자예요. (Juh-neun chae-sheeg-jjoo-eui-jah-yeah-yoh.)

□ **Do you have anything with no <u>meat</u> in it?**

JDM: <u>고기</u> 안 들어간 음식 있나요? (<u>Goh-ghee</u> ahn deu-ruh-gah neum-shee gheet-nah-yoh?)

□ **I can't eat spicy food / I can't handle spicy food**

JDM: 매운 음식은 못 먹어요. (Mae-woo neum-shee-geun moht muh-guh-yoh.)

□ **Spicy food is fine / I like spicy food**

JDM: 매운 거 잘 먹어요. (Mae-woon guh jahl muh-guh-yoh.)

☐ Is this spicy?

JDM: 이거 매워요? (Ee-guh mae-wuh-yoh?)

☐ How spicy is this?

JDM: 이거 얼마나 매워요? (Ee-guh uhl-mah-nah mae-wuh-yoh?)

☐ I'll have this / I'd like to order this

JDM: 이거 주세요. (Ee-guh joo-seh-yoh.)

☐ I'll have the same / Me, too

JDM: 저도요. (Juh-doh-yoh.)

☐ I'd like <u>coke</u> with it / And a <u>coke</u>, please

JDM: 콜라도 같이 주세요. (<u>Cohl-lah</u>-doh gah-chee joo-seh-yoh.)

*같이 (gah-chee) = together

☐ It's for to go / To go, please

JDM: 포장해 주세요. (Poh-jahng-hae joo-seh-yoh.)

□ How do I eat this?

JDM: 이건 어떻게 먹어요? (Ee-guh nuh-dduh-keh muh-guh-yoh?)

□ I don't think I can eat this / I don't want to eat it

JDM: 못 먹겠어요. (Moht muhg-ggeh-ssuh-yoh.)

□ Excuse me / Over here, please

JDM: 저기요. (Juh-ghee-yoh.)

□ Can I get a glass of water?

JDM: 물 좀 주시겠어요? (Mool johm joo-shee-geh-ssuh-yoh?)

□ Do you happen to have a <u>fork</u>?

JDM: 혹시 <u>포크</u> 있으신가요? (Hohg-ssee <u>poh-keu</u> ee-sseu-sheen-gah-yoh?)

*혹시 (hohg-ssee) = perhaps

□ I need some <u>napkins</u> / Can I get some <u>napkins</u>?

JDM: <u>휴지</u> 좀 주세요.(<u>Hyou-jee</u> johm joo-seh-yoh.)

□ Check, please / We're ready to pay

JDM: 계산서요. (Gyeah-sahn-suh-yoh.)

*Some restaurants may not give out checks or bills

□ I'm buying tonight / Let me get the check

JDM: 오늘은 제가 낼게요. (Oh-neu-reun jeh-gah nael-ggeh-yoh.)

□ Do you have a doggy bag? / Can I get a container for the leftover?

JDM: 남은 거 싸갈 수 있나요? (Nah-meun guh ssah-gahl ssoo eet-nah-yoh?)

10. Hotels

□ I'd like to check in, please

JDM: 체크인이요. (Cheh-keu-ee-nee-yoh.)

□ I'd like a room / One room, please

JDM: 방 하나요. (Bahng hah-nah-yoh.)

*방 (bahng) = room

□ I'd like to reserve a room

JDM: 방 하나 예약이요. (Bahng hah-nah yeah-yah-ghee-yoh.)

□ Do you have a vacant room?

JDM: 빈 방 있나요? (Been bahng eet-nah-yoh?)

□ How many beds are in the room?

JDM: 방에 침대가 몇 대예요? (Bahng-eh cheem-dae-gah myuht ddae-yeah-yoh?)

*침대 (cheem-dae) = bed

☐ I'd like a room with <u>2 beds</u>

JDM: <u>2인실</u>로 주세요. (<u>Ee-een-sheel</u>-loh joo-seh-yoh.)

☐ Do you have any deluxe rooms?

JDM: 특실이 있으신가요? (Teug-ssee-ree ee-sseu-sheen-gah-yoh?)

*특실 (teug-sseel) = deluxe room/suite room

☐ I'll be staying for <u>2 days</u>

JDM: <u>2일</u> 동안 머물 거예요. (<u>Ee-eel</u> ddohng-ahn muh-mool gguh-yeah-yoh.)

☐ How much is it per night?

JDM: 하루에 얼마예요? (Hah-roo-eh uhl-mah-yeah-yoh?)

☐ What is the lowest price?

JDM: 제일 저렴한 게 얼마예요? (Jeh-eel juh-ryuhm-hahn geh uhl-mah-yeah-yoh?)

☐ Do you have room service?

JDM: 룸서비스 돼요? (Room-ssuh-bee-sseu dwae-yoh?)

□ **Is breakfast included?**

JDM: 아침식사도 포함인가요? (Ah-cheem-sheeg-ssah-doh poh-hah-meen-gah-yoh?)

*아침식사 (ah-cheem-sheeg-ssah) = breakfast

□ **Is there breakfast? / Do you provide breakfast?**

JDM: 아침식사 나오나요? (Ah-cheem-sheeg-ssah nah-oh-nah-yoh?)

□ **Is <u>Wi-Fi</u> extra?**

JDM: <u>인터넷</u>은 따로 돈 내나요? (<u>Een-tuh-neh</u>-seun ddah-roh dohn nae-nah-yoh?)

□ What time is the check-out?

JDM: 체크아웃은 몇시까지 인가요? (Cheh-keu-ah-woo-seun myuht-ssee-ggah-jee een-gah-yoh?)

□ Can I get a wake-up call?

JDM: 모닝콜 해주실 수 있나요? (Moh-ning-kohl hae-joo-sheel ssoo eet-nah-yoh?)

*모닝콜 (moh-ning-kohl) = wake-up call

□ I'd like a new bedsheet

JDM: 침대 시트 좀 바꿔 주세요 (Cheem-dae shee-teu johm bah-ggwuh joo-seh-yoh.)

□ What time is breakfast?

JDM: 아침식사는 몇시인가요? (Ah-cheem-sheeg-ssah-neun myuht-ssee-een-gah-yoh?)

□ I've lost my key / I'm locked out of the room

JDM: 키를 잃어버렸어요. (Kee-reu ree-ruh-buh-ryuh-ssuh-yoh.)

□ I'd like to switch the room / Can I get another room?

JDM: 방을 바꿀 수 있나요? (Bahng-eul bah-ggool ssoo eet-nah-yoh?)

□ I'd like to check out now

JDM: 체크아웃이요. (Cheh-keu-ah-woo-shee-yoh.)

□ Can you call a taxi, please? / Can you get a taxi for me?

JDM: 택시 불러 주실 수 있나요? (Taeg-ssee bool-luh joo-sheel ssoo eet-nah-yoh?)

11. Time & Dates

☐ What time is it? / Do you have the time?

JDM: 지금 몇 시예요? (Jee-geum myuht ssee-yeah-yoh?)

BM: 지금 몇 시야? (Jee-geum myuht ssee-yah?)

*지금 (jee-geum) = right now

☐ Is this the right time?

JDM: 이거 맞는 시간인가요? (Ee-guh maht-neun shee-gah-neen-gah-yoh?)

BM: 이거 맞는 시간이니? (Ee-guh maht-neun shee-gah-nee-nee?)

*시간 (shee-gahn) = time/hour

☐ I'll be there in <u>2 hours</u> / I'm arriving in <u>2 hours</u>

JDM: <u>2시간</u> 안에 도착할 거예요. (<u>Doo-shee-gah</u> nah-neh doh-chah-kahl gguh-yeah-yoh.)

BM: <u>2시간</u> 안에 도착할 거야. (<u>Doo-shee-gah</u> nah-neh doh-chah-kahl gguh-yah.)

☐ I'll be arriving at <u>3</u> / The plane lands at <u>3 o'clock</u>

JDM: <u>3시</u> 도착이에요. (<u>Seh-shee</u> doh-chah-ghee-eh-yoh.)

BM: 3시 도착이야. (<u>Seh-shee</u> doh-chah-ghee-yah.)

*도착 (doh-chahg) = arrival

□ It says 'July 9th at <u>10 a.m.</u>' / It's July 9th at <u>10 a.m.</u>

JDM: 7월 9일 <u>오전 10시</u>요. (Chee-rwuhl goo-ee <u>roh-juh nyuhl-ssee</u>-yoh.)

BM: 7월 9일 <u>오전 10시</u>. (Chee-rwuhl goo-ee <u>roh-juh nyuhl-ssee</u>.)

*오전 (oh-juhn) = a.m.

□ Let's meet at <u>8:30 at night</u> / Meet me at <u>8:30 p.m.</u>

JDM: <u>오후 8시 반</u>에 만나요. (<u>Oh-hoo yuh-duhl-ssee bah</u>-neh mahn-nah-yoh.)

BM: <u>오후 8시 반</u>에 만나자. (<u>Oh-hoo yuh-duhl-ssee bah</u>-neh mahn-nah-jah.)

*오후 (oh-hoo) = p.m.

□ What day is it today?

JDM: 오늘이 무슨 요일이에요? (Oh-neu-ree moo-seu nyoh-ee-ree-eh-yoh?)

BM: 오늘이 무슨 요일이야? (Oh-neu-ree moo-seu nyoh-ee-ree-yah?)

*오늘 (oh-neul) = today

□ Is today <u>Wednesday</u>?

JDM: 오늘이 <u>수요일</u>이에요? (Oh-neu-ree <u>soo-yoh-ee</u>-ree-eh-yoh?)

BM: 오늘이 <u>수요일</u>이야? (Oh-neu-ree <u>soo-yoh-ee</u>-ree-yah?)

☐ I'm going to stay here for <u>6 months</u>

JDM: <u>6개월</u> 동안 있을 거예요. (<u>Youg-ggae-wuhl</u> ddohng-ah nee-sseul gguh-yeah-yoh.)

BM: <u>6개월</u> 동안 있을 거야. (<u>Youg-ggae-wuhl</u> ddohng-ah nee-sseul gguh-yah.)

☐ I leave on <u>August 25th</u> / I go home on <u>August 25th</u>

JDM: <u>8월 25일</u>에 떠나요. (<u>Pah-rwuh ree-shee-boh-ee</u>-reh dduh-nah-yoh.)

BM: <u>8월 25일</u>에 떠나. (<u>Pah-rwuh ree-shee-boh-ee</u>-reh dduh-nah.)

*떠나다 (dduh-nah-dah) = leave/go

☐ Can I see you <u>next week</u>?

JDM: <u>다음 주</u>에 뵐 수 있을까요? (<u>Dah-eum jjoo</u>-eh bwehl ssoo ee-sseul-ggah-yoh?)

BM: <u>다음 주</u>에 만날 수 있어? (<u>Dah-eum jjoo</u>-eh mahn-nahl ssoo ee-ssuh?)

☐ <u>Monday</u> is good / I'm free on <u>Monday</u>

JDM: <u>월요일</u> 괜찮아요. (<u>Wuh-ryoh-ee</u>l gwaen-chah-nah-yoh.)

BM: <u>월요일</u> 괜찮아. (<u>Wuh-ryoh-ee</u>l gwaen-chah-nah.)

□ <u>Friday</u> is no good / I can't make it on <u>Friday</u>

JDM: <u>금요일</u>은 안 돼요. (<u>Geu-myoh-ee</u>-reu nahn dwae-yoh.)

BM: <u>금요일</u>은 안 돼. (<u>Geu-myoh-ee</u>-reu nahn dwae.)

□ Are you free on <u>Saturday</u>? / Do you have time on <u>Saturday</u>?

JDM: <u>토요일</u>에 시간 있으세요? (<u>Toh-yoh-ee</u>-reh shee-gah nee-sseu-seh-yoh?)

BM: <u>토요일</u>에 시간 있어? (<u>Toh-yoh-ee</u>-reh shee-gah nee-ssuh?)

□ I'm staying here only for a while / I won't be here for long

JDM: 잠시만 머물 거예요. (Jahm-shee-mahn muh-mool gguh-yeah-yoh.)

BM: 잠시만 머물 거야. (Jahm-shee-mahn muh-mool gguh-yah.)

*머물다 (muh-mool-dah) = stay

□ I've already made plans for the weekend / I'm busy this weekend

JDM: 주말에 약속이 있어요. (Joo-mah-reh yahg-ssoh-ghee ee-ssuh-yoh.)

BM: 주말에 약속이 있어. (Joo-mah-reh yahg-ssoh-ghee ee-ssuh.)

*주말 (joo-mahl) = weekend

12. Weather & Seasons

□ It's sunny / It's a clear day

JDM: 날이 맑네요. (Nah-ree mahg-neh-yoh.)

BM: 날이 맑다. (Nah-ree mahg-ddah.)

*날 (nahl) = day

□ It's raining

JDM: 비 와요. (Bee wah-yoh.)

BM: 비 와. (Bee wah.)

*비 (bee) = rain

□ It's snowing

JDM: 눈 내려요. (Noon nae-ryuh-yoh.)

BM: 눈 내린다. (Noon nae-reen-dah.)

*눈 (noon) = snow

☐ I think it's going to <u>rain</u>

JDM: <u>비</u> 올 거 같아요. (<u>Bee</u> ohl gguh gah-tah-yoh.)

BM: <u>비</u> 올 거 같아. (<u>Bee</u> ohl gguh gah-tah.)

☐ It's going to <u>snow</u> tomorrow

JDM: 내일 <u>눈</u> 온대요. (Nae-eel <u>noo</u> nohn-dae-yoh.)

BM: 내일 <u>눈</u> 온대.(Nae-eel <u>noo</u> nohn-dae.)

*내일 (nae-eel) = tomorrow

☐ Is it raining outside?

JDM: 밖에 비 와요? (Bah-ggeh bee wah-yoh?)

BM: 밖에 비 와? (Bah-ggeh bee wah?)

□ How's the weather in <u>London</u>?

JDM: 런던에 날씨는 어때요? (<u>Ruhn-duh</u>-neh nahl-ssee-neu nuh-ddae-yoh?)

BM: 런던 날씨는 어때? (<u>Ruhn-duhn</u> nahl-ssee-neu nuh-ddae?)

*날씨 (nahl-ssee) = weather

□ The weather is good

JDM: 날씨 좋아요. (Nahl-ssee joh-ah-yoh.)

BM: 날씨 좋아. (Nahl-ssee joh-ah-yoh.)

□ The weather is bad

JDM: 날씨 안 좋아요. (Nahl-ssee ahn joh-ah-yoh.)

BM: 날씨 안 좋아. (Nahl-ssee ahn joh-ah.)

□ It rains a lot in <u>June</u>

JDM: <u>6월</u>에는 비가 많이 와요. (<u>You-wuh</u>-reh-neun bee-gah mah-nee wah-yoh.)

BM: <u>6월</u>에는 비가 많이 와. (<u>You-wuh</u>-reh-neun bee-gah mah-nee wah.)

□ It never snows in <u>Florida</u> / We don't get snow in <u>Florida</u>

JDM: <u>플로리다</u>에는 눈 안 와요. (<u>Peul-loh-ree-dah</u>-eh-neun noo nah nwah-yoh.)

BM: <u>플로리다</u>에는 눈 안 와. (<u>Peul-loh-ree-dah</u>-eh-neun noo nah nwah.)

□ What is your favorite season? / Which season do you like the most?

JDM: 어떤 계절을 제일 좋아하세요? (Uh-dduhn gyeah-juh-reul jeh-eel joh-ah-hah-seh-yoh?)

BM: 어떤 계절이 제일 좋아? (Uh-dduhn gyeah-juh-ree jeh-eel joh-ah?)

*계절 (gyeah-juhl) = season

□ I like <u>spring</u> / I love <u>spring</u>

JDM: 전 <u>봄</u>을 좋아해요. (Juhn <u>boh</u>-meul joh-ah-hae-yoh.)

BM: 난 <u>봄</u>이 좋아. (Nahn <u>boh</u>-mee joh-ah.)

□ <u>Summer</u> is the best / <u>Summer</u> is my favorite season

JDM: <u>여름</u>이 제일 좋아요. (<u>Yuh-reu</u>-mee jeh-eel joh-ah-yoh.)

BM: <u>여름</u>이 제일 좋아. (<u>Yuh-reu</u>-mee jeh-eel joh-ah.)

□ I don't like <u>autumn</u> / I hate <u>fall</u>

JDM: <u>가을</u>은 별로 안 좋아해요. (<u>Gah-eu</u>-reun byuhl-loh ahn joh-ah-hae-yoh.)

BM: <u>가을</u>은 별로 안 좋아해. (<u>Gah-eu</u>-reun byuhl-loh ahn joh-ah-hae.)

□ Do you like <u>winter</u>?

JDM: <u>겨울</u> 좋아하세요? (<u>Gyuh-wool</u> joh-ah-hah-seh-yoh?)

BM: <u>겨울</u> 좋아해? (<u>Gyuh-wool</u> joh-ah-hae?)

□ It's too hot

JDM: 너무 더워요. (Nuh-moo duh-wuh-yoh.)

BM: 너무 더워. (Nuh-moo duh-wuh.)

*덥다 (duhb-ddah) = hot

□ It's too cold

JDM: 너무 추워요. (Nuh-moo choo-wuh-yoh.)

BM: 너무 추워. (Nuh-moo choo-wuh.)

*춥다 (choob-ddah) = cold

□ It's a little chilly

JDM: 날이 좀 쌀쌀해요. (Nah-ree johm ssahl-ssahl-hae-yoh.)

BM: 날이 좀 쌀쌀하네. (Nah-ree johm ssahl-ssahl-hah-neh.)

*좀 (johm) = little

□ What is the current temperature?

JDM: 지금 몇 도예요? (Jee-geum myuht ddoh-yeah-yoh?)

BM: 지금 몇 도야? (Jee-geum myuht ddoh-yah?)

*도 (doh) = degree

☐ It's 35 degrees

JDM: 35도예요. (Sahm-shee-boh-doh-yeah-yoh.)

BM: 35도. (Sahm-shee-boh-doh.)

☐ Is it in Celsius?

JDM: 섭씨로요? (Suhb-ssee-roh-yoh?)

BM: 섭씨로? (Suhb-ssee-roh?)

☐ What is it in Celsius?

JDM: 섭씨로는 몇 도예요? (Suhb-ssee-roh-neun myuht ddoh-yeah-yoh?)

BM: 섭씨로는 몇 도야? (Suhb-ssee-roh-neun myuht ddoh-yah?)

*섭씨 (suhb-ssee) = Celsius (℃)

☐ What is it in Fahrenheit?

JDM: 화씨로는 몇 도예요? (Hwah-ssee-roh-neun myuht ddoh-yeah-yoh?)

BM: 화씨로는 몇 도야? (Hwah-ssee-roh-neun myuht ddoh-yah?)

*화씨 (hwah-ssee) = Fahrenheit (℉)

13. Phone Conversations

□ Hello?

JDM: 여보세요? (Yuh-boh-seh-yoh?)

□ May I ask who's calling? / Sorry, who is this?

JDM: 실례지만 누구세요? (Sheel-lyeah-jee-mahn noo-goo-seh-yoh?)

□ This is <u>John</u> speaking

JDM: 저 존입니다. (Juh <u>joh</u>-neeb-nee-dah.)

BM: 나 존이야. (Nah <u>joh</u>-nee-yah.)

YES, THIS IS ZORRO

HOW DARE YOU CALL ME

☐ May I speak to <u>Dohee</u>?

JDM: <u>도희</u>랑 통화할 수 있나요? (<u>Doh-dee</u>-rahng tohng-hwah-hahl ssoo eet-nah-yoh?)

BM: <u>도희</u> 좀 바꿔 줄래? (<u>Doh-hee</u> johm bah-ggwuh jool-lae?)

☐ Please hold / Just one moment

JDM: 잠시만요. (Jahm-shee-mah-nyoh.)

BM: 잠깐만. (Jahm-ggahn-mahn.)

☐ Can I put you on hold?

JDM: 잠시만 기다려 주시겠어요? (Jahm-shee-mahn ghee-dah-ryuh joo-shee-geh-ssuh-yoh?)

BM: 잠시만 기다려 줄래? (Jahm-shee-mahn ghee-dah-ryuh jool-lae?)

☐ I'm sorry, I think I've got the wrong number

JDM: 죄송합니다, 전화 잘못 걸었어요. (Jweh-sohng-hahb-nee-dah, juhn-hwah jahl-moht guh-ruh-ssuh-yoh.)

☐ Wrong number / You called a wrong number

JDM: 전화 잘못 거셨습니다. (Juhn-hwah jahl-moht gguh-shuht-sseub-nee-dah.)

☐ I'm calling from a public phone

JDM: 공중전화로 했어요. (Gohng-joong-juhn-hwah-roh hae-ssuh-yoh.)

BM: 공중전화로 했어. (Gohng-joong-juhn-hwah-roh hae-ssuh.)

*공중전화 (gohng-joong-juhn-hwah) = public phone

□ He's not here / He's not in right now

JDM: 지금 안 계세요. (Jee-geu mahn gyeah-seh-yoh.)

BM: 지금 없어. (Jee-geu muhb-ssuh.)

*지금 (jee-geum) = right now

□ She can't come to the phone right now / She's busy right now

JDM: 지금 전화 받으실 수 없어요. (Jee-geum juhn-hwah bah-deu-sheel ssoo uhb-ssuh-yoh.)

BM: 지금 전화 못 받아. (Jee-geum juhn-hwah moht bbah-dah.)

□ Would you like to leave a message?

JDM: 혹시 남기실 말씀 있으세요? (Hohg-ssee nahm-ghee-sheel mahl-sseu mee-sseu-seh-yoh?)

□ Can I leave a message?

JDM: 말 좀 전달해 주시겠어요? (Mahl johm juhn-dahl-hae joo-shee-geh-ssuh-yoh?)

□ The number you have dialed is not in service

JDM: 지금 거신 전화번호는 없는 번호입니다. (Jee-geum guh-sheen juhn-hwah-buhn-hoh-neu nuhb-neun buhn-hoh-eeb-nee-dah.)

☐ I'm sorry, can you repeat that? / Sorry?

JDM: 죄송한데 다시 한번 말씀해 주시겠어요? (Jweh-sohng-hahn-deh dah-shee hahn-buhn mahl-sseum-hae joo-shee-geh-ssuh-yoh?)

*다시 한번 (dah-shee hahn-buhn) = one more time

☐ I don't understand what you're saying

JDM: 무슨 말씀인지 모르겠어요. (Moo-seun mahl-sseu-meen-jee moh-reu-geh-ssuh-yoh.)

☐ I'll call back later / Let me call back

JDM: 다시 전화 드릴게요. (Dah-shee juhn-hwah deu-reel-ggeh-yoh.)

*다시 (dah-shee) = again

☐ Is there someone who speaks English?

JDM: 영어 할 수 있는 사람 있나요? (Yuhng-uh hahl ssoo eet-neun sah-rah meet-nah-yoh?)

☐ When should I call back?

JDM: 언제 전화 드리면 되죠? (Uhn-jeh juhn-hwah deu-ree-myuhn dweh-jyoh?)

☐ Thanks for the call / Thank you for calling

JDM: 전화 주셔서 감사합니다. (Juhn-hwah joo-shuh-suh gahm-sah-hahb-nee-dah.)

BM: 전화 고마워. (Juhn-hwah goh-mah-wuh.)

□ I'll tell him you called

JDM: 전화 하셨다고 말씀 드릴게요. (Juhn-hwah hah-shuht-ddah-goh mahl-sseum deu-reel-ggeh-yoh.)

BM: 전화 했다고 얘기 할게. (Juhn-hwah haet-ddah-goh yaeh-ghee hahl-ggeh.)

14. K-pop & Entertainment

☐ I like K-pop / I love K-pop

JDM: 전 케이팝 좋아해요. (Juhn keh-ee-pahb jjoh-ah-hae-yoh.)

BM: 난 케이팝 좋아해. (Nahn keh-ee-pahb jjoh-ah-hae.)

*좋아하다 (joh-ah-hah-dah) = like/love

☐ I listen to K-pop

JDM: 전 케이팝 들어요. (Juhn keh-ee-pahb ddeu-ruh-yoh.)

BM: 난 케이팝 들어. (Nahn keh-ee-pahb ddeu-ruh.)

☐ I don't listen to K-pop

JDM: 전 케이팝 잘 안 들어요. (Juhn keh-ee-pahb jjah rahn deu-ruh-yoh.)

BM: 난 케이팝 잘 안 들어. (Nahn keh-ee-pahb jjah rahn deu-ruh.)

☐ I like to watch K-pop music videos

JDM: 케이팝 뮤직비디오 보는 걸 좋아해요. (Keh-ee-pahb myou-jeeg-bbee-dee-oh boh-neun guhl joh-ah-hae-yoh.)

BM: 케이팝 뮤직비디오 보는 걸 좋아해. (Keh-ee-pahb myou-jeeg-bbee-dee-oh boh-neun guhl joh-ah-hae.)

□ I like to dance / I love dancing

JDM: 춤추는 거 좋아해요. (Choom-choo-neun guh joh-ah-hae-yoh.)

BM: 춤추는 거 좋아해. (Choom-choo-neun guh joh-ah-hae.)

*춤추다 (choom-choo-dah) = dance

□ Do you like K-pop?

JDM: 케이팝 좋아하세요? (Keh-ee-pahb jjoh-ah-hah-seh-yoh?)

BM: 너 케이팝 좋아해? (Nuh keh-ee-pahb jjoh-ah-hae?)

□ What is your favorite K-pop group?

JDM: 케이팝 그룹 누구 좋아하세요? (Keh-ee-pahb ggeu-roub noo-goo joh-ah-hah-seh-yoh?)

BM: 케이팝 그룹 누구 좋아해? (Keh-ee-pahb ggeu-roub noo-goo joh-ah-hae?)

□ Who is your favorite K-pop singer?

JDM: 케이팝 가수 누구 좋아하세요? (Keh-ee-pahb ggah-soo noo-goo joh-ah-hah-seh-yoh?)

BM: 케이팝 가수 누구 좋아해? (Keh-ee-pahb ggah-soo noo-goo joh-ah-hae?)

가수 (gah-soo) = singer

□ I'm a fan of Jihoon

JDM: 전 지훈 팬이에요. (Juhn jee-hoon pae-nee-eh-yoh.)

BM: 난 지훈 팬이야. (Nahn jee-hoon pae-nee-yah.)

□ I'm a fan / I'm your fan

JDM: 저 팬이에요. (Juh pae-nee-eh-yoh.)

□ Can I get your autograph?

JDM: 싸인 해주실래요? (Ssah-een hae-joo-sheel-lae-yoh?)

☐ Can I take a photo with you? / Can we take a picture?

JDM: 같이 사진 찍어도 돼요? (Gah-chee sah-jeen jjee-guh-doh dwae-yoh?)

*사진 (sah-jeen) = photo

☐ I have your album / I bought your album

JDM: 저 앨범 있어요. (Juh ael-buh mee-ssuh-yoh.)

☐ I came here to see you / I'm here to see you

JDM: 보려고 왔어요. (Boh-ryuh-goh wah-ssuh-yoh.)

*보다 (boh-dah) = see

☐ I really like your new song

JDM: 신곡 진짜 좋아요. (Sheen-gohg jeen-jjah joh-ah-yoh.)

*신곡 (sheen-gohg) = newly-released song

☐ I want to see 9KOREA

JDM: 9코리아 보고 싶어요. (Nah-een-koh-ree-ah boh-goh shee-puh-yoh.)

BM: 9코리아 보고 싶어. (Nah-een-koh-ree-ah boh-goh shee-puh.)

□ I want to go to <u>9KOREA's concert</u>

JDM: <u>9코리아 콘서트</u> 가고 싶어요. (<u>Nah-een-koh-ree-ah kohn-ssuh-teu</u> gah-goh shee-puh-yoh.)

BM: <u>9코리아 콘서트</u> 가고 싶어. (<u>Nah-een-koh-ree-ah kohn-ssuh-teu</u> gah-goh shee-puh.)

□ I'm going to <u>9KOREA's concert</u>

JDM: <u>9코리아 콘서트</u> 갈 거예요. (<u>Nah-een-koh-ree-ah kohn-ssuh-teu</u> gahl gguh-yeah-yoh.)

BM: <u>9코리아 콘서트</u> 갈 거야. (<u>Nah-een-koh-ree-ah kohn-ssuh-teu</u> gahl gguh-yah.)

□ I like <u>10KOREA</u> better

JDM: 전 <u>10코리아</u> 더 좋아해요. (Juhn <u>tehn-koh-ree-ah</u> duh joh-ah-hae-yoh.)

BM: 난 <u>10코리아</u> 더 좋아해. (Nahn <u>tehn-koh-ree-ah</u> duh joh-ah-hae.)

*더 (duh) = more/better

□ I love Korean <u>musicals</u>

JDM: 한국 <u>뮤지컬</u> 좋아해요. (Hahn-goong <u>myou-jee-kuhl</u> joh-ah-hae-yoh.)

BM: 한국 <u>뮤지컬</u> 좋아해. (Hahn-goong <u>myou-jee-kuhl</u> joh-ah-hae.)

*한국 (hahn-goog) = Korea/Korean

□ I'm into K-dramas / I like watching K-dramas

JDM: 한국 드라마 재밌어요. (Hahn-goog ddeu-rah-mah jae-mee-ssuh-yoh.)

BM: 한국 드라마 재밌어. (Hahn-goog ddeu-rah-mah jae-mee-ssuh.)

□ Do you watch K-dramas?

JDM: 한국 드라마 보세요? (Hahn-goog ddeu-rah-mah boh-seh-yoh?)

BM: 한국 드라마 봐? (Hahn-goog ddeu-rah-mah bwah?)

□ I watch <u>Soomba Got Married</u> / <u>Soomba Got Married</u> is my favorite K-drama

JDM: <u>숨바가 결혼했다</u> 보고 있어요. (<u>Soom-bah-gah gyuhl-hohn-haet-ddah</u> boh-goh ee-ssuh-yoh.)

BM: <u>숨바가 결혼했다</u> 봐. (<u>Soom-bah-gah gyuhl-hohn-haet-ddah</u> bwah.)

□ <u>Zorro Returns</u> is my favorite Korean movie

JDM: <u>조로 리턴즈</u>가 제일 재밌었어요. (<u>Joh-roh ree-tuhn-jeu</u>-gah jae-eel jae-mee-ssuh-ssuh-yoh.)

BM: <u>조로 리턴즈</u>가 제일 재밌었어. (<u>Joh-roh ree-tuhn-jeu</u>-gah jeh-eel jae-mee-ssuh-ssuh.)

☐ Do you want to see <u>Zorro Returns</u>?

JDM: <u>조로 리턴즈</u> 보실래요? (<u>Joh-roh ree-tuhn-jeu</u> boh-sheel-lae-yoh?)

BM: <u>조로 리턴즈</u> 볼래? (<u>Joh-roh ree-tuhn-jeu</u> bohl-lae?)

☐ I saw <u>Zorro Returns</u> / I've already seen <u>Zorro Returns</u>

JDM: <u>조로 리턴즈</u> 봤어요. (<u>Joh-roh ree-tuhn-jeu</u> bwah-ssuh-yoh.)

BM: <u>조로 리턴즈</u> 봤어. (<u>Joh-roh ree-tuhn-jeu</u> bwah-ssuh.)

15. Education

☐ Class starts at <u>7:30</u>

JDM: 수업은 <u>7시 반</u>에 시작합니다.(Soo-uh-beu <u>neel-gohb-ssee bah</u>-neh shee-jah-kahb-nee-dah.)

BM: 수업은 <u>7시 반</u>에 시작해. (Soo-uh-beu <u>neel-gohb-ssee bah</u>-neh shee-jah-kae.)

*수업 (soo-uhb) = class

☐ I go to <u>Ganada School</u>

JDM: 저 <u>가나다학교</u> 다녀요. (Juh <u>gah-nah-dah-hahg-ggyoh</u> dah-nyuh-yoh.)

BM: 나 <u>가나다학교</u> 다녀. (Nah <u>gah-nah-dah-hahg-ggyoh</u> dah-nyuh.)

☐ I'm in <u>10th grade</u>

JDM: <u>10학년</u>이에요. (<u>Shee-pahg-nyuh</u>-nee-eh-yoh.)

BM: <u>10학년</u>이야. (<u>Shee-pahg-nyuh</u>-nee-yah.)

☐ Teacher, I have a question

JDM: 선생님, 질문 있어요. (Suhn-saeng-neem, jeel-moo nee-ssuh-yoh.)

*질문 (jeel-moon) = question

□ I've finished my homework

JDM: 숙제 다 했어요. (Soog-jjeh dah hae-ssuh-yoh.)

BM: 숙제 다 했어. (Soog-jjeh dah hae-ssuh.)

*숙제 (soog-jjeh) = homework

□ We have a test tomorrow

JDM: 내일 시험 있어요. (Nae-eel shee-huh mee-ssuh-yoh.)

BM: 내일 시험 있어. (Nae-eel shee-huh mee-ssuh.)

*시험 (shee-huhm) = test/exam

□ I did well on the test

JDM: 시험 잘 봤어요. (Shee-huhm jahl bwah-ssuh-yoh.)

BM: 시험 잘 봤어. (Shee-huhm jahl bwah-ssuh.)

□ I did poorly on the test

JDM: 시험 잘 못 봤어요. (Shee-huhm jahl moht bwah-ssuh-yoh.)

BM: 시험 잘 못 봤어. (Shee-huhm jahl moht bwah-ssuh.)

☐ I passed the test

JDM: 시험에 합격했어요. (Shee-huh-meh hahb-ggyuh-kae-ssuh-yoh.)

BM: 시험 합격했어. (Shee-huhm hahb-ggyuh-kae-ssuh.)

☐ I failed the test

JDM: 시험에 떨어졌어요. (Shee-huh-meh dduh-ruh-juh-ssuh-yoh.)

BM: 시험 떨어졌어. (Shee-huhm dduh-ruh-juh-ssuh.)

☐ <u>English</u> is my favorite subject / I like <u>English</u> the best

JDM: <u>영어</u>가 제일 재밌어요. (<u>Yuhng-uh</u>-gah jeh-eel jae-mee-ssuh-yoh.)

BM: <u>영어</u>가 제일 재밌어. (<u>Yuhng-uh</u>-gah jeh-eel jae-mee-ssuh.)

☐ I like <u>math</u> the least / <u>Math</u> is my least favorite subject

JDM: <u>수학</u>이 제일 별로예요. (<u>Soo-hah</u>-ghee jeh-eel byuhl-loh-yeah-yoh.)

BM: <u>수학</u>이 제일 별로야. (<u>Soo-hah</u>-ghee jeh-eel byuhl-loh-yah.)

☐ Can I borrow a <u>pencil</u>?

JDM: <u>연필</u> 좀 빌릴 수 있을까요? (<u>Yuhn-peel</u> johm beel-leel ssoo ee-sseul-ggah-yoh?)

BM: <u>연필</u> 좀 빌려줄래? (<u>Yuhn-peel</u> johm beel-lyuh-jool-lae?)

*빌리다 (beel-lee-dah) = borrow

☐ What does this word mean?

JDM: 이 단어의 뜻이 뭐예요? (Ee dah-nuh-eui ddeu-shee mwuh-yeah-yoh?)

BM: 이 단어 뜻이 뭐야? (Ee dah-nuh ddeu-shee mwuh-yah?)

*단어 (dah-nuh) = word

☐ My dog ate my homework

JDM: 개가 숙제를 먹었어요. (Gae-gah soog-jjeh-reul muh-guh-ssuh-yoh.)

BM: 개가 숙제를 먹었어. (Gae-gah soog-jjeh-reul muh-guh-ssuh.)

*개 (gae) = dog

16. Job Interviews

□ Here is my résumé / This is my résumé

JDM: 제 이력서입니다. (Jeh ee-ryuhg-ssuh-eeb-nee-dah.)

*이력서 (ee-ryuhg-ssuh) = résumé

□ I have <u>2 years</u> of experience

JDM: 경력이 <u>2년</u> 있습니다. (Gyuhng-nyuh-ghee <u>ee-nyuh</u> neet-sseub-nee-dah.)

*경력 (gyuhng-nyuhg) = experience

□ I went to <u>Soomba University</u> / I graduated from <u>Soomba University</u>

JDM: <u>숨바대</u>를 나왔습니다. (<u>Soom-bah-dae</u>-reul nah-waht-sseub-nee-dah.)

*대 (dae) = College/University

□ I majored in <u>history</u> / <u>History</u> was my major

JDM: 전공은 <u>역사</u>입니다. (Juhn-gohng-eu <u>nhuhg-ssah</u>-eeb-nee-dah.)

*전공 (juhn-gohng) = major

☐ I have no criminal record

JDM: 전과는 없습니다. (Juhn-ggwah-neu nuhb-sseub-nee-dah.)

*전과 (juhn-ggwah) = criminal record

☐ I'm a fast learner / I learn quickly

JDM: 저는 빨리 배우는 편이에요. (Juh-neun bbahl-lee bae-woo-neun pyuh-nee-eh-yoh.)

*빨리 (bbahl-lee) = quickly/fast

☐ I speak 3 languages

JDM: 3개 국어를 합니다. (Sahm-gae goo-guh-reul hahb-nee-dah.)

*국어 (goo-guh) = languages

□ I speak <u>English</u>, <u>Spanish</u>, and <u>Japanese</u>

JDM: 저는 영어, 스페인어, 일본어를 합니다. (Juh-neu <u>nyuhng-uh</u>, <u>seu-peh-ee-nuh</u>, <u>eel-boh-nuh</u>-reul hahb-nee-dah.)

□ I'd like to know more about the position

JDM: 직책에 대해 더 알고 싶습니다. (Jeeg-chae-geh dae-hae duh ahl-goh sheep-sseub-nee-dah.)

*직책 (jeeg-chaeg) = position

□ What are the working hours?

JDM: 근무 시간은 어떻게 되나요? (Geun-moo shee-gah-neu nuh-dduh-keh dweh-nah-yoh?)

*근무 시간 (geun-moo shee-gahn) = working hours

□ May I ask you about the salary?

JDM: 급여에 대해 질문드려도 될까요? (Geu-byuh-eh dae-hae jeel-moon-deu-ryuh-doh dwehl-ggah-yoh?)

*급여 (geu-byuh) = salary

□ Is the salary negotiable?

JDM: 급여는 협상이 가능한가요? (Geu-byuh-neun hyuhb-ssahng-ee gah-neung-hahn-gah-yoh?)

□ Thank you for seeing me / Thank you for the interview

JDM: 불러 주셔서 감사합니다. (Bool-luh joo-shuh-suh gahm-sah-hahb-nee-dah.)

17. Hospitals & Pharmacies

□ I think I have a <u>cold</u>

JDM: <u>감기</u>인 거 같아요. (<u>Gahm-ghee</u>-een guh gah-tah-yoh.)

BM: <u>감기</u>인 거 같아. (<u>Gahm-ghee</u>-een guh gah-tah.)

□ I'm looking for a <u>dentist</u>

JDM: <u>치과</u>를 찾고 있어요. (<u>Chee-ggwah</u>-reul chaht-ggoh ee-ssuh-yoh.)

BM: <u>치과</u> 찾고 있어. (<u>Chee-ggwah</u> chaht-ggoh ee-ssuh.)

□ Can you recommend me an <u>acupuncturist</u>?

JDM: <u>한의원</u> 잘하는 데 아세요? (<u>Hah-neui-wuhn</u> jahl-hah-neun deh ah-seh-yoh?)

BM: <u>한의원</u> 잘하는 데 알아? (<u>Hah-neui-wuhn</u> jahl-hah-neun deh ah-rah?)

□ **I have an appointment for 5:30**

JDM: 5시 반 예약이요. (Dah-suht-ssee bah nyeah-yah-ghee-yoh.)

*예약 (yeah-yahg) = appointment

□ **I don't have an appointment**

JDM: 예약 안 했는데요. (Yeah-yah gahn haet-neun-deh-yoh.)

□ **Do I need to make an appointment?**

JDM: 예약해야 되나요? (Yeah-yah-kae-yah dweh-nah-yoh?)

□ I'd like to make an appointment

JDM: 예약해 주세요. (Yeah-yah-kae joo-seh-yoh.)

□ I'd like to cancel my appointment

JDM: 예약 취소할게요. (Yeah-yahg chwee-soh-hahl-ggeh-yoh.)

*취소하다 (chwee-soh-hah-dah) = cancel

□ Do I need insurance?

JDM: 보험이 있어야 하나요? (Boh-huh-mee ee-ssuh-yah hah-nah-yoh?)

*보험 (boh-huhm) = insurance

□ Where can I get insurance?

JDM: 보험은 어디서 신청해요? (Boh-huh-meu nuh-dee-suh sheen-chuhng-hae-yoh?)

□ Does the doctor speak English?

JDM: 의사선생님 영어 하세요? (Eui-sah-suhn-saeng-nee myuhng-uh hah-seh-yoh?)

*의사선생님 (eui-sah-suhn-saeng-neem) = doctor

□ Do you have anyone who speaks English?

JDM: 영어 하시는 분 있나요? (Yuhng-uh hah-shee-neun boo neet-nah-yoh?)

□ I'm currently taking <u>amphetamine</u>

JDM: <u>암페타민</u> 복용하고 있어요. (<u>Ahm-peh-tah-meen</u> boh-gyohng-hah-goh ee-ssuh-yoh.)

□ I'm allergic to <u>penicillin</u>

JDM: 저는 <u>페니실린</u> 알레르기가 있어요. (Juh-neun <u>peh-nee-sheel-lee</u> nahl-leh-reu-ghee-gah ee-ssuh-yoh.)

*알레르기 (ahl-leh-reu-ghee) = allergy

115

□ Do you have anything for <u>stomach pain</u>?

JDM: <u>배 아픈데</u> 먹는 약 있어요? (Bae ah-peun-deh muhg-neu nyah ghee-ssuh-yoh?)

□ Can I get a box of <u>Band-Aid</u>? / One box of <u>Band-Aid</u>, please

JDM: <u>반창고</u> 하나 주세요. (Bahn-chahng-goh hah-nah joo-seh-yoh.)

□ Do you have a <u>first aid kit</u>?

JDM: <u>구급상자</u> 있어요? (<u>Goo-geub-ssahng-jah</u> ee-ssuh-yoh?)

□ Does this have any side effects?

JDM: 부작용 있나요? (Boo-jah-gyohng eet-nah-yoh?)

*부작용 (boo-jah-gyohng) = side effect

□ I'm afraid of needles

JDM: 전 주사가 무서워요. (Juhn joo-sah-gah moo-suh-wuh-yoh.)

BM: 난 주사가 무서워. (Nahn joo-sah-gah moo-suh-wuh.)

*주사 (joo-sah) = syringe/needle

□ My blood type is <u>O negative</u>

JDM: 제 혈액형은 <u>오 마이너스</u>예요. (Jeh hyuh-rae-kyuhng-eu <u>noh mah-ee-nuh-sseu</u>-yeah-yoh.)

BM: 내 혈액형은 <u>오 마이너스</u>야. (Nae hyuh-rae-kyuhng-eu <u>noh mah-ee-nuh-sseu</u>-yah.)

*혈액형 (hyuh-rae-kyuhng) = blood type

□ I don't know my blood type

JDM: 저 혈액형 몰라요. (Juh hyuh-rae-kyuhng mohl-lah-yoh.)

BM: 나 혈액형 몰라. (Nah hyuh-rae-kyuhng mohl-lah.)

18. Emergencies

□ This is an emergency / It's an emergency

JDM: 위급 상황이에요. (Wee-geub ssahng-hwahng-ee-eh-yoh.)

□ Somebody call 119 / Can someone please dial 119?

JDM: 누가 119에 전화 좀 해주세요. (Noo-gah eel-leel-goo-eh juhn-hwah johm hae-joo-seh-yoh.)

*Dial 119 anywhere in South Korea for emergency situations

□ Help! / Help me, please!

JDM: 도와주세요! (Doh-wah-joo-seh-yoh!)

□ We need an ambulance / Please send an ambulance

JDM: 구급차가 필요해요. (Goo-geub-chah-gah pee-ryoh-hae-yoh.)

*구급차 (goo-geub-chah) = ambulance

□ Please hurry

JDM: 빨리 오세요. (Bbahl-lee oh-seh-yoh.)

□ I need a doctor right away

JDM: 의사가 빨리 필요해요. (Eui-sah-gah bbahl-lee pee-ryoh-hae-yoh.)

*의사 (eui-sah) = doctor

□ I can't breathe / I have trouble breathing

JDM: 숨을 잘 못 쉬겠어요. (Soo-meul jahl moht sswee-geh-ssuh-yoh.)

□ We have an accident / There is an accident

JDM: 사고가 났어요. (Sah-goh-gah nah-ssuh-yoh.)

*사고 (sah-goh) = accident

□ I'm seriously injured / I got hurt badly

JDM: 제가 심하게 다쳤어요. (Jeh-gah sheem-hah-geh dah-chuh-ssuh-yoh.)

□ Someone is passed out

JDM: 누가 기절했어요. (Noo-gah ghee-juhl-hae-ssuh-yoh.)

*누가 (noo-gah) = someone

□ Someone has been hit by a car

JDM: 누가 자동차에 치였어요. (Noo-gah jah-dohng-chah-eh chee-yuh-ssuh-yoh.)

*자동차 (jah-dohng-chah) = car/automobile

□ Fire! / The building is on fire!

JDM: 불이야! (Boo-ree-yah!)

□ We have a fire / The house is on fire

JDM: 불이 났어요. (Boo-ree nah-ssuh-yoh.)

□ There is a suspicious person

JDM: 수상한 사람이 있어요. (Soo-sahng-hahn sah-rah-mee ee-ssuh-yoh.)

*수상하다 (soo-sahng-hah-dah) = suspicious

□ Someone is trying to break into my place

JDM: 누가 집에 침입하려고 해요. (Noo-gah jee-beh chee-mee-pah-ryuh-goh hae-yoh.)

□ I've been attacked / Someone attacked me

JDM: 폭행을 당했어요. (Poh-kaeng-eul dahng-hae-ssuh-yoh.)

□ Somebody took my <u>wallet</u> / My <u>wallet</u> is stolen

JDM: 누가 제 <u>지갑</u>을 훔쳐 갔어요. (Noo-gah jeh <u>jee-gah</u>-beul hoom-chuh gah-ssuh-yoh.)

□ I've been robbed / My place has been robbed

JDM: 도둑이 들었어요. (Doh-doo-ghee deu-ruh-ssuh-yoh.)

*도둑 (doh-doog) = thief/burglar

19. Common Korean Phrases

Here is a list of common Korean phrases used by many Korean speakers. (Whereas the previous chapters are for helping you express yourself in Korean, this chapter is for listening and comprehension.)

Commands & Requests

JDM: 잠시만요. (Jahm-shee-mah-nyoh.)

BM: 잠시만. (Jahm-shee-mahn.)

= Hold on / Wait a second

JDM: 한 번만요. (Hahn buhn-mah-nyoh.)

BM: 한 번만. (Hahn buhn-mahn.)

= Please? / Come on

JDM: 하지 마세요. (Hah-jee mah-seh-yoh.)

BM: 하지 마. (Hah-jee mah.)

= Don't do that / Don't

JDM: 그만 하세요. (Geu-mahn hah-seh-yoh.)

BM: 그만 해. (Geu-mahn hae.)

= That's enough / Please stop

JDM: 안 돼요. (Ahn dwae-yoh.)

BM: 안 돼. (Ahn dwae.)

= No / No, I can't / I don't want to

Compliments

JDM: 멋있어요. (Muh-shee-ssuh-yoh.)

BM: 멋있다. (Muh-sheet-ddah.)

= You look handsome / It looks nice

JDM: 잘 생겼어요. (Jahl saeng-gyuh-ssuh-yoh.)

BM: 잘 생겼다. (Jahl saeng-gyuht-ddah.)

= You're a good-looking guy / What a handsome guy

JDM: 예뻐요. (Yeah-bbuh-yoh.)

BM: 예쁘다. (Yeah-bbeu-dah.)

= You're pretty / It looks pretty

JDM: 잘하셨어요. (Jahl-hah-shuh-ssuh-yoh.)

BM: 잘했어. (Jahl-hae-ssuh.)

= Good job / Nice work

JDM: 맛있어요. (Mah-shee-ssuh-yoh.)

BM: 맛있어. (Mah-shee-ssuh.)

= It's delicious / It's very tasty

Descriptions

JDM: 있어요. (Ee-ssuh-yoh.)

BM: 있어. (Ee-ssuh.)

= I have it / Yes, she's here

JDM: 없어요. (Uhb-ssuh-yoh.)

BM: 없어. (Uhb-ssuh.)

= I don't have it / No, he's not here

JDM: 많아요. (Mah-nah-yoh.)

BM: 많아. (Mah-nah.)

= There's a lot / I have a lot

JDM: 적어요. (Juh-guh-yoh.)

BM: 적어. (Juh-guh.)

= There's not a lot / We don't have a lot

JDM: 진짜예요. (Jeen-jjah-yeah-yoh.)

BM: 진짜야. (Jeen-jjah-yah.)

= It's true / It's real

JDM: 좋아요. (Joh-ah-yoh.)

BM: 좋아. (Joh-ah.)

= It's good / It's pretty good

JDM: 별로예요. (Byuhl-loh-yeah-yoh.)

BM: 별로야. (Byuhl-loh-yeah.)

= It's not that great / It's okay

Emotions & Feelings

JDM: 좋아해요. (Joh-ah-hae-yoh.)

BM: 좋아해. (Joh-ah-hae.)

= I like you / I like it / I love it

JDM: 사랑해요. (Sah-rahng-hae-yoh.)

BM: 사랑해. (Sah-rahng-hae.)

= I love you / I'm in love with you

JDM: 행복해요. (Haeng-boh-kae-yoh.)

BM: 행복해. (Haeng-boh-kae.)

= I'm happy

JDM: 싫어요. (Shee-ruh-yoh.)

BM: 싫어. (Shee-ruh.)

= I don't want to / I don't like it

JDM: 죄송해요. (Jweh-sohng-hae-yoh.)

BM: 미안해. (Mee-ahn-hae.)

= I'm sorry / I'm really sorry

JDM: 재밌어요. (Jae-mee-ssuh-yoh.)

BM: 재밌어. (Jae-mee-ssuh.)

= It's really fun / It's very interesting

JDM: 신기해요. (Sheen-ghee-hae-yoh.)

BM: 신기하다. (Sheen-ghee-hah-dah.)

= I've never seen something like this before

JDM: 아까워요. (Ah-ggah-wuh-yoh.)

BM: 아까워. (Ah-ggah-wuh.)

= What a waste / It's such a waste

JDM: 힘들어요. (Heem-deu-ruh-yoh.)

BM: 힘들어. (Heem-deu-ruh.)

= I'm tired / It's hard / It's not that easy

JDM: 죽겠어요. (Joog-ggeh-ssuh-yoh.)

BM: 죽겠다. (Joog-ggeht-ddah.)

= I'm dying / I'm losing my mind

JDM: 피곤해요. (Pee-gohn-hae-yoh.)

BM: 피곤해. (Pee-gohn-hae.)

= I'm tired / I'm exhausted / I'm all worn out

JDM: 졸려요. (Johl-lyuh-yoh.)

BM: 졸려. (Johl-lyuh.)

= I feel sleepy / I want to go to bed

JDM: 어머나! (Uh-muh-nah!)

BM: 어머나! (Uh-muh-nah!)

= Oh my! / Ah!

JDM: 어떡해. (Uh-dduh-kae.)

BM: 어떡해. (Uh-dduh-kae.)

= Oh no / Uh oh / What should I do?

JDM: 아이고. (Ah-ee-goh.)

BM: 아이고. (Ah-ee-goh.)

= Wow / Awesome / All right / Oh / Darn it / Shoot

Greetings & Customs

JDM: 어서 오세요. (Uh-suh oh-seh-yoh.)

BM: 어서 와. (Uh-suh wah.)

= Come in already / Hi

JDM: 오셨어요? (Oh-shuh-ssuh-yoh?)

BM: 왔어? (Wah-ssuh?)

= Hey, you're here / Hi

JDM: 반갑습니다. (Bahn-gahb-sseub-nee-dah.)

BM: 반갑다. (Bahn-gahb-ddah.)

= Nice to meet you / I'm glad to meet you

JDM: 식사는 하셨어요? (Sheeg-ssah-neun hah-shuh-ssuh-yoh?)

BM: 밥 먹었어? (Bahb muh-guh-ssuh?)

= Did you eat? / What's up? / How are you?

JDM: 일어나셨어요? (Ee-ruh-nah-shuh-ssuh-yoh?)

BM: 일어났어? (Ee-ruh-nah-ssuh?)

= You're awake / Did you sleep well? / Good morning

JDM: 조심히 들어가세요. (Joh-sheem-hee deu-ruh-gah-seh-yoh.)

BM: 조심히 들어가. (Joh-sheem-hee deu-ruh-gah.)

= Get home safely / Be careful on your way home / Bye

JDM: 수고하세요. (Soo-goh-hah-seh-yoh.)

BM: 수고해. (Soo-goh-hae.)

= Work hard / Thanks, bye

JDM: 잘 먹겠습니다. (Jahl muhg-ggeht-sseub-nee-dah.)

BM: 잘 먹을게. (Jahl muh-geul-ggeh.)

= I'll eat well / Let's dig in / Let me have some of this

JDM: 잘 먹었습니다. (Jahl muh-guht-sseub-nee-dah.)

BM: 잘 먹었어. (Jahl muh-guh-ssuh.)

= I ate well / I enjoyed the meal / Thank you for the meal

Opinions & Statements

JDM: 할 줄 알아요. (Hahl jjoo rah-rah-yoh.)

BM: 할 줄 알아. (Hahl jjoo rah-rah.)

= I know how to do it / I can do it

JDM: 할 줄 몰라요. (Hahl jjool mohl-lah-yoh.)

BM: 할 줄 몰라. (Hahl jjool mohl-lah.)

= I don't know how to do it / I can't do it

JDM: 잘해요. (Jahl-hae-yoh.)

BM: 잘해. (Jahl-hae.)

= I'm good at it / I'm pretty good

JDM: 잘 못 해요. (Jahl moh tae-yoh.)

BM: 잘 못 해. (Jahl moh tae.)

= I'm not good at it / I'm not that good

JDM: 쉬워요. (Shwee-wuh-yoh.)

BM: 쉬워. (Shwee-wuh.)

= It's easy

JDM: 어려워요. (Uh-ryuh-wuh-yoh.)

BM: 어려워. (Uh-ryuh-wuh.)

= It's difficult

JDM: 가 봤어요. (Gah bwah-ssuh-yoh.)

BM: 가 봤어. (Gah bwah-ssuh.)

= Yes, I've been there before

JDM: 못 가 봤어요. (Moht ggah bwah-ssuh-yoh.)

BM: 못 가 봤어. (Moht ggah bwah-ssuh.)

= No, I've never been there before

JDM: 저도 그렇게 생각해요. (Juh-doh geu-ruh-keh saeng-gah-kae-yoh.)

BM: 나도 그렇게 생각해. (Nah-doh geu-ruh-keh saeng-gah-kae.)

= I think so, too / I agree

JDM: 잘 모르겠어요. (Jahl moh-reu-geh-ssuh-yoh.)

BM: 잘 모르겠어. (Jahl moh-reu-geh-ssuh.)

= I'm not sure / I don't understand / I'm confused

JDM: 몰랐어요. (Mohl-lah-ssuh-yoh.)

BM: 몰랐어. (Mohl-lah-ssuh.)

= I didn't know that / I had no idea

JDM: 생각 안 나요. (Saeng-gah gahn nah-yoh.)

BM: 생각 안 나. (Saeng-gah gahn nah.)

= I can't remember / I don't recall

Responses

JDM: 네, 알겠습니다. (Neh, ahl-geht-sseub-nee-dah.)

BM: 어, 알았어. (Uh, ah-rah-ssuh.)

= Okay / All right / Got it

JDM: 네, 그래요. (Neh, geu-rae-yoh.)

BM: 어, 그래. (Uh, geu-rae.)

= Yes, okay / Sure, why not?

JDM: 네, 맞아요. (Neh, mah-jah-yoh.)

BM: 어, 맞아. (Uh, mah-jah.)

= Yes / That's right / You're right

JDM: 아뇨. (Ah-nyoh.)

BM: 아니. (Ah-nee.)

= No

JDM: 네, 알아요. (Neh, ah-rah-yoh.)

BM: 어, 알아. (Uh, ah-rah.)

= Yes, I know

JDM: 아뇨, 몰라요. (Ah-nyoh, mohl-lah-yoh.)

BM: 아니, 몰라. (Ah-nee, mohl-lah.)

= No, I don't know

JDM: 네, 좋아요. (Neh, joh-ah-yoh.)

BM: 어, 좋아. (Uh, joh-ah.)

= Yes, sure / Yeah, okay

JDM: 아뇨, 괜찮아요. (Ah-nyoh, gwaen-chah-nah-yoh.)

BM: 아냐, 괜찮아. (Ah-nyah, gwaen-chah-nah.)

= No, I'm fine / No, it's okay / No, thank you

JDM: 네, 있어요. (Neh, ee-ssuh-yoh.)

BM: 어, 있어. (Uh, ee-ssuh.)

= Yes, I have it

JDM: 아뇨, 없어요. (Ah-nyoh, uhb-ssuh-yoh.)

BM: 아니, 없어. (Ah-nee, uhb-ssuh.)

= No, I don't have it

JDM: 그런 거 같아요. (Geu-ruhn guh gah-tah-yoh.)

BM: 그런 거 같아. (Geu-ruhn guh gah-tah.)

= I think so / Probably

JDM: 아닌 거 같아요. (Ah-neen guh gah-tah-yoh.)

BM: 아닌 거 같아. (Ah-neen guh gah-tah.)

= I don't think so / Probably not

JDM: 맞아요. (Mah-jah-yoh.)

BM: 맞아. (Mah-jah.)

= You're right / That's right

JDM: 아니에요. (Ah-nee-eh-yoh.)

BM: 아니야. (Ah-nee-yah.)

= No, you're wrong

JDM: 그럴까요? (Geu-ruhl-ggah-yoh?)

BM: 그럴까? (Geu-ruhl-ggah?)

= Yes, why not? / Sure / Okay

JDM: 그러니까요. (Geu-ruh-nee-ggah-yoh.)

BM: 그러니까. (Geu-ruh-nee-ggah.)

= Exactly / Tell me about it

JDM: 그럼요. (Geu-ruh-myoh.)

BM: 그럼. (Geu-ruhm.)

= Of course / Sure, sure

JDM: 설마요. (Suhl-mah-yoh.)

BM: 설마. (Suhl-mah.)

= That can't be / No way / I hope not

JDM: 다음에요. (Dah-eu-meh-yoh.)

BM: 다음에. (Dah-eu-meh.)

= Maybe next time / Maybe later

JDM: 말도 안 돼요. (Mahl-doh ahn dwae-yoh.)

BM: 말도 안 돼. (Mahl-doh ahn dwae.)

= No way / That's unbelievable

Questions

JDM: 왜요? (Wae-yoh?)

BM: 왜? (Wae?)

= Why? / What? / What happened?

JDM: 뭐가요? (Mwuh-gah-yoh?)

BM: 뭐가? (Mwuh-gah?)

= What do you mean? / What?

JDM: 맞아요? (Mah-jah-yoh?)

BM: 맞아? (Mah-jah?)

= Is it true? / Is that right?

JDM: 아니에요? (Ah-nee-eh-yoh?)

BM: 아니야? (Ah-nee-yah?)

= No? / Am I wrong? / Isn't it?

JDM: 정말이에요? (Juhng-mah-ree-eh-yoh?)

BM: 정말? (Juhng-mahl?)

= Really? / Seriously?

JDM: 진짜요? (Jeen-jjah-yoh?)

BM: 진짜? (Jeen-jjah?)

= Are you serious? / Really?

20. Common English Words

Many Korean speakers understand and use English words on a daily basis. Since most of these words are nouns, you can form simple Korean sentences by combining them with Korean verbs. (To get a list of basic Korean verbs and more, check out Korean Words with Cat Memes 2/5.) This means you can talk to people in Korean at a very basic level even if you are not familiar with many Korean words. Here are some English words and expressions that most Korean speakers understand.

General Phrases

nice to meet you, oh my God, very good, happy birthday, see you next time, I don't know

Questions

who, what, where, when, why, how, how many, how much

Air & Travel

airplane, airport, passport, bag, train, subway, car, ship, taxi, bus

Directions

left, right, go, come, corner, map, straight, turn

Numbers

number words (1 ~ 99), hundred, thousand, plus, minus, double, half

Money & Banks

dollar, pay, cash, credit card, bank

Shopping

shoe, bag, skirt, pants, shirt, tie, necklace, sock, ring, gold, silver

Food & Restaurants

menu, order, steak, fork, spoon, soup, napkin, seafood, cup, restaurant

Hotels

check-in, check-out, key, front desk, room, bed, towel

Time & Dates

hour, minute, second, day, week, weekend, month, year

Weather & Seasons

summer, winter, cold, hot, rain, snow, cloud, sky, sunny, star

Phone Conversations

telephone, telephone number, call, message, text message

K-pop & Entertainment

singer, musician, fan, star, artist, band, song, music, movie, comedy, concert, museum

Education

school, student, teacher, pencil, pen, paper, eraser, desk, chair, blackboard, class, classroom, test

Job Interviews

job, work, interview, office, boss, intern, meeting

Hospitals & Pharmacies

hospital, doctor, nurse, blood, medicine, body, heart, skin

Emergencies

ambulance, fire, 911 (119), help

Hangul Pronunciations

Hangul Consonants

ㄱ = g/k   ㄴ = n   ㄷ = d   ㄹ = l/r   ㅁ = m

ㅂ = b   ㅅ = s/sh   ㅇ = o   ㅈ = j   ㅊ = ch

ㅋ = k   ㅌ = t   ㅍ = p   ㅎ = h   ㄲ = gg/kk

ㄸ = dd/tt   ㅃ = bb   ㅆ = ss   ㅉ = jj

Hangul Vowels

ㅏ = ah   ㅑ = yah   ㅓ = uh   ㅕ = yuh

ㅗ = oh   ㅛ = yoh   ㅜ = woo   ㅠ = you

ㅐ = ae   ㅒ = yaeh   ㅔ = eh   ㅖ = yeah

ㅘ = wah   ㅙ = wae   ㅚ = weh

ㅝ = wuh   ㅞ = weah   ㅟ = wee

ㅡ = eu   ㅣ = yee   ㅢ = eui

More Books

Korean Grammar with Cat Memes

Basic Korean Grammar for beginners

Basic Hangul guide

Cat memes of Soomba and Zorro

Available in eBook and paperback formats

Korean Words with Cat Memes (1 ~ 5)

250+ essential words (per book) for beginners

Example sentences in English and Hangul

Cat memes of Soomba and Zorro

Available in eBook and paperback formats

More Information

EASY KOREAN

Visit www.easy-korean.com for free Korean lessons, dictionary, and more.

EASY KOREAN on YouTube

Access grammar, listening, vocabulary, and hangul videos for beginners.

EASY KOREAN on Twitter (@EASY_KOREAN)

Follow EASY KOREAN on Twitter and get the latest updates.

9KOREA - Get Korea in English

Visit www.9korea.com for articles and more on living in Korea.

About the Author

Min Kim is the creator of EASY KOREAN among other projects. He was born in South Korea but spent his teenage years in the United States. He currently lives in Seoul with his two cats, Soomba and Zorro.

If you found this book helpful, please leave a review on the place of purchase. Thank you.

M.K.

Made in the USA
Columbia, SC
31 October 2019